LEADING THE WAY

LEADERSHIP IS NOT JUST FOR SUPER CHRISTIANS

PAUL BORTHWICK

Waynesboro, Georgia USA

Published by Gabriel Publishing
PO Box 1047, 129 Mobilization Dr
Waynesboro, GA 30830 U.S.A.
(706) 554-1594
gabriel@omlit.om.org

ISBN: 1-884543-87-1

Cover design: Paul Lewis

Printed in Colombia
Impreso en Colombia

CONTENTS

Introduction 5
Acknowledgement 9
Foreword 10
The Challenge for Young Leaders 13

Part One: The Marks of a Leader 25
1. What You Say 37
2. What You Do 61
3. The Impact of Love 81
4. Building Your Faith 101
5. A Commitment to Purity 131

Part Two: The Resources of a Leader 151
6. Enthusiasm for God 155
7. Applying Your Knowledge 167
8. The Right Kind of Idealism 181
9. More Experienced Leaders 195

Conclusion: The Challenge of the Future 215
Notes 221
Appendix A: Literature for Leaders 235
Appendix B: Young Leaders' Agenda 241

INTRODUCTION

When I first wrote *Leading the Way*, my wife, Christie, and I were part of a group of young men and women who were being targeted as "younger leaders." Older people who led churches, schools and mission organizations encouraged us about our potential, rebuked us for our reticence to lead, and exhorted us to "take up the torch" to lead the church into this new millennium. (It was from this group that Gordon Aeschliman drafted the "Young Leader Agenda" which appears in Appendix B of this book.)

As these veteran leaders stirred us to rise to the challenge of leading the church, I began asking the question, "What is leadership?" and especially, "What distinguishes Christian leadership?" The research lead to this book.

In contrast to some of the trends, I became convinced that developing Christian leadership is

NOT just some sort of "How To" manual, although manuals can assist the process;

NOT motivational psychology baptized in Christian jargon, although motivational stories throughout the Bible and Christian history do help us;

NOT the design of prescribed programs, although programs can assist the process.

If you're looking for how-tos and programs, you'll be disappointed with this book! Leadership is deeper than manuals and programs. It's far more than being excited about a vision statement or motivating others to join us. Instead, leadership flows from our personal lives. Christian leaders' personal lives are their greatest assets. Issues like calling and vision and ministry all flow from a dedication to pursue Christlike character. Who we are precedes our ability to lead.

As you read *Leading The Way*, you'll hear three basic messages, messages that we now take with us as we serve to encourage leaders across the world.

LEAD BY EXAMPLE

Peter Kusmic of Croatia stated that "charisma without character is catastrophe." Many leaders fall prey to the temptation to lead by power, by charisma, or simply by position. Biblical leadership is saying to others:

- "Follow me" - as with Jesus (Matthew 4:19) and Paul (I Corinthians 11:1).
- "Look at my life" - as with Paul in Philippians 4:9.
- "Watch the way I live" - as with Jesus (John 13) and Paul (I Thessalonians 2:9).

This is why the first half of this book is built on I Timothy 4:12 which calls us to lead by example in the most crucial issues of character: speech, conduct, love, faith, purity. Leadership through power or position is hollow. It's the power of an exemplary life that truly influences others towards the kingdom.

GROW THROUGH YOUR PAIN

Many of us "younger leaders" who received the challenges years ago did not realize how much of leadership character gets forged in the fires of pain. When we meet men and women who did rise to the challenge to undertake leadership, we don't need to dig too deeply before we encounter their pain. Hurts accumulate through years of ministry. Chronic physical hardship or relational tension often lingers in the lives of the people God uses.

One of the messages in this book simply stated is: don't waste your pain! The poem in Chapter 10 about being "hammered and hurt" in the process of growth is true for the men and women we meet who are being effectively used by God. They grow and minister through and beyond their pain.

Pain can lead to bitterness (this isn't fair!). Or pain can lead to passion, which in the Greek literally means "to suffer." Passion is desiring something so much that we'd be willing to suffer or die for it, like Paul's "one thing I do" in Philippians 3. Without being glib or superficial about the reality of pain, long-term leaders are often those who allow God to turn their pains into passion for Christ and His kingdom.

STAY IN THE RACE

Many leaders suffer from encouragement-deprivation, a common disease in long-term ministry. Drawing on our own Boston heritage, we allude to the Boston

Marathon as an illustration of the Christian life. Staying in the race is the goal; finishing is the prize.

Perhaps the best message we can learn from "More Experienced Leaders" (Chapter 9) comes from Hebrews 12:1-3. Don't forget all of those who've gone before you (the Hebrews 11 legends of faith) and fix your eyes on Jesus. He awaits you at the Finish Line with the message, "Well done, good and faithful servant."

My prayer is that this book will encourage you to lead through your character, to grow through your pain, and to stay in the race that Jesus Christ has laid out for you.

ACKNOWLEDGMENTS

If it should seem presumptuous for me to write from the assumption that I—like my readers—am aspiring toward leadership, I must confess that it is not totally my fault. In some respects, I aspire toward leadership because others have believed in me in the process of my growth.

In the early days of my Christian walk, my dad, along with key others including Sam Hollo, Emie Tavilla, Lyle Jacobson, Warren Schuh, and Lyle Mook, played a very significant role in challenging me toward leadership responsibilities.

Without a doubt, Gordon MacDonald has been the most influential person on my leadership growth through his encouragement, rebuke, and coaching. There are many others to add to this list: J. Christy Wilson, Bob Ludwig, Dan Dustin, and Bob Wessel have been older leaders who set examples for me to follow. Tim Conder, Steve Macchia, Mary Ann Mitchener, and Doug Whallon have been fellow young leaders in the process with me.

I am also deeply grateful to Leighton Ford for his encouragement to me and to many other aspiring younger leaders. Above all others, however, my wife, Christie, continues to be the most significant gift of God to me to stir me in the process of growth. I thank God for her love, her commitment to making me a better man, and the life we share. I dedicate this book to her.

FOREWORD

Most of us are naturally drawn to people who like what we like. I, for example, gravitate readily to those who admire the University of North Carolina Tarheels in basketball, golden retrievers as pets, John Stott as a preacher, and those who think my wife and children are the greatest! (My favorite expositor and my family obviously belong in a totally different category than dogs!)

When I learned that Paul Borthwick was writing a book on younger leadership, I was inclined to be receptive. The twin passions of my heart and life are: to communicate Christ with relevance, integrity, and creativity to our world; to identify, develop, and network younger leaders for the same cause.

Leading the Way: Leadership Is Not Just for Super Christians is timely because we are now in a worldwide leadership transition. The world, and especially the followers of Christ, should be waiting for and waving on the emerging generation of leaders.

Now, after reading Paul's book, I am even more inclined to recommend it. *Leading the Way* is bold, balanced, believable:

- bold, in that it correctly assesses the critical challenges of our day and urges young leaders to take the steps that will enable them to be and do all that God calls them to be and do;

- balanced, because Paul seeks to write both from a biblical and a contemporary perspective, and to keep charisma and character, public ministry, and personal maturity in tension;
- believable, because Paul focuses both on the pain and fulfillment of leadership and honestly illustrates the process of leadership development based on the challenges, the stretching, the questions, the failures and successes that have been part of his own growth.

The veteran Apostle Paul obviously had great stakes in the development of his protégé Timothy and great joy when he saw Timothy growing and serving with him as a son in the gospel. Something of the same feeling is mine when, as an older brother, I see a younger man such as Paul Borthwick reaching out to be a faithful leader in Christ. I recommend *Leading the Way* to the young leaders we work with in our own ministry. I believe both senior and younger leaders will benefit from reading it. I pray that Paul Borthwick and his generation may be able to faithfully model what he has so well written.

LEIGHTON FORD

The Challenge for Young Leaders

A LOOK AT OUR TIMES

Across the world, people are concerned about the apparent dearth of leadership in the younger generation. As Christian leaders from the past generation near or reach retirement, their cry goes forth, "Who will take the lead now?" "Where are the leaders?"

Doug Whallon, regional director for InterVarsity Christian Fellowship, reports the findings of InterVarsity's Donald Posterski that "young people today hunger for friendship and simultaneously *avoid leadership*." Whallon observes that the challenge of developing leaders is intensifying because there are few students with a strong enough Christian grounding to step into roles of Christian leadership; the interest in leadership simply isn't there; and cultural leadership and Kingdom leadership are increasingly different in content and style.[1]

While Doug Whallon is referring to the Christian world in general and the audience of InterVarsity in particular, the "leadership vacuum" phenomenon is not unique to the Christian world. Secular writers, sociologists, and futurists are observing what one author calls the "postponed generation,"[2] a generation that is avoiding the responsibilities of adult life by perpetuating its adolescent-type behaviors. One manifestation of this leadership vacuum in the academic world was reported in *U.S. News and World Report* by Gordon Fee of the University of Colorado. He stated that "in the seven years between 1973-74 and 1980-81, the proportion of faculty members over the age of 50 increased from 31.3% to 42%, while those under 35 decreased from 20.3% to 6.3%. The Carnegie Council on Policy Studies in Higher Education has estimated that by about the year 2000, professors over age 46 will constitute 65% of all faculty members."[3] Fee is raising the question: Where are the young people who will lead in the academic world?

Many young people in their twenties and thirties are entering adult life disillusioned, apathetic, or bored. Some suffer from a deluded "sense of entitlement", a feeling that life owes them something; that there is a utopia to be found out there without commitment and cost.

Others suffer the accumulated disillusionment of years of media influence. They grew up thinking that life would be as wonderful as it is portrayed in the movies or on television. When they find that, as M. Scott Peck says in *The Road Less Traveled,*[4] "Life is difficult," they grow hostile, withdrawn, or cynical.

Donald McCullough addresses this reaction in his

book *Waking from the American Dream*. The result of unfulfilled dreams or a harsh introduction to the realities of adult life "is often depression or despair. Depression occurs with an inner loss, with the loss of one's self. Despair occurs with an outer loss, with the loss of part of one's world. Depression destroys concern ('I just don't care anymore'), and despair destroys hope ('the world is going to hell in a handbasket')."[5]

In general, we are a generation that wants the rewards of adult life without doing the hard work and commitment required to get them. A single friend of mine described his version of the perfect woman and the perfect marriage, but his description included nothing about the hard work, hours of communication, and long-term commitment that a healthy marriage needs. My friend will either remain single, or he will get married to his dream woman, only to be disillusioned to find that a good marriage does not just "happen."

In trying to help young people understand the depression or despair that they begin to experience about the responsibilities of adult life, I explain that life is similar to a travel brochure. When we look at the pictures, the descriptions, and the enticing promises of a travel brochure, we want to sign up immediately for the vacation offered. But there is an asterisk: *Special Restrictions Apply.

What does it mean? It means that the real trip may not live up to our expectations created by the brochure; it will cost more, or it will not be quite as glamorous as the brochure promises. The beautiful beaches do exist, but they are crowded with fellow tourists and vendors;

the ski slopes feature virgin snow at times, but it may be packed hard by the time we get there.

The young person who feels that adult life is not as idyllic as expected is starting to read the warning: *Special Restrictions Apply! Rewards in life take work. Relationships require commitment. Leadership means risk-taking and the willingness to stand alone. McCullough expands on this theme in *Waking from the American Dream*:

> We live in a culture that tells us our dreams can be realized with enough hard work and positive thinking. But at one time or another, in one way or another, we wake up to reality. We learn, often with great pain, that we can't always have what we desperately want. Perhaps a marriage leaves us lonelier than we thought possible, or a single life feels like an inescapable prison, or sexual drives remain frustrated, or vocational advancement has been blocked, or health evades us, or God seems to have locked himself in an unresponsive heaven—disappointment comes in a variety of ways, and it can send us straight into the pit.[6]

Perhaps the saddest response of the young adult to the disillusionment of life and the realities of "Special Restrictions" was summed up by a friend who told me he aspires only to "move to a desert island in the South

Pacific to be left alone." His despairing response reflected his own fear of life and his feeling that he could not make any difference.

Old age might be defined as the time when our memories of things past exceed our dreams of things to come. As such, old age can be a state of mind, a state that my escapist friend had already entered at age twenty-nine. He wanted to retreat and reminisce about the "good ol' days" of high school, college, and dazzling romances. Thoughts of the future were preoccupied with fear and best avoided.

Two generations ago, the Beatles called young people to change the world through revolution, a revolution in which "all you need is love." The current generation—those who should be taking up the reins of leadership in society and in the church—do not believe it. The spirit of pessimism or hopelessness or selfishness seems to have taken over. Changing the world is not on the agenda of many young adults.

THE NEED CONTINUES

Fear of the future and the unwillingness of young adults to take the lead in society or in the church—for whatever reasons—does not diminish the reality of the current need for leadership. We live in an age like that described in Judges 21:25, where "everyone did as he saw fit." Leadership has become relative; everyone wanders because there is no unifying vision (see Proverbs 29:18).

But in the midst of it all, older leaders are calling for younger men and women who will respond to the call to leadership in these challenging times. The Lausanne Committee for World Evangelization is asking, "Who will guide the church for the next forty years?" Dr. Ted Engstrom of World Vision International exhorts young leaders to take the passed baton of leadership in his book *Seizing the Torch.*[7] Dr. John Stott concludes his two-volume work entitled *Involvement* with a "Call for Christian Leadership," an appeal directed at young leaders to respond to the global, social, moral, and spiritual crises of our age.[8]

The challenges are great, but God's call is greater. In the same way that Paul, the older Christian leader, challenged Timothy, the younger, potential leader, we need to hear the call of God to

- *preach the Word* (understanding our times and applying God's Word to them);
- *be prepared in season and out of season* (even when the culture has become relativistic or barren of leadership, we must be ready for action);
- *correct, rebuke, and encourage* (taking on the challenge of leadership by teaching and leading others; 2 Timothy 4:2).

As we enter a new millennium, there is a vacuum of leadership. The need is felt *now* for young men and women who will rise to the challenge—in the face of great opportunities and great obstacles—to be obedient to the call to leadership.

WHY SHOULD I RESPOND?

Whenever I hear a call to leadership, I want to affirm the need for leaders who will pay the price, make the sacrifices, and fight the battles necessary to lead in our world. But I have a difficult time seeing how I fit into the picture. My instinctive response is, "Yes, Lord, we need leaders.... Please send *someone else.*"

I am reminded of a teenager in a Bible study I once led. At one meeting he shared his Bible with me. In the margins I noticed many names. I asked him why they were there. His response: "Those are people I thought verses applied to."

He was happy to apply the rebukes and commands of the Scriptures to someone else, but he had not considered applying them to himself.

We may be inclined to do the same. We may think, "Yes, we need young men and women who will offer Christian leadership in the Church, in business, in our communities, in science, in technology, etc. I wonder *who else* God wants to send?" The premise of this book is that God wants to send *you* and *me*. *We* must rise to the challenge of leadership. *We* are called by God to provide the vision and exemplary lifestyles that our world needs. *We* are called to the commitments, sacrifices, and servanthood required of leaders.

There are indeed many difficult issues that the Church and society will face. To be a leader may sound glamorous, but as we see the realities of our world we will know—*Special Restrictions Apply. In spite of all of these restrictions, however, God calls us to respond.

WE RESPOND BECAUSE IT'S BIBLICAL

Some of us shrink away from the challenge of leadership by appealing to humility. We say, "I could never be a leader," or "Only God can make a leader; for me to think of myself as a leader is presumptuous."

These responses reflect a genuine desire to be humble, but they do not take into account the affirmations of Scripture. In the Sermon on the Mount, Jesus referred to His followers as the "salt of the earth" and the "light of the world." His implication? That those who follow Him are the instruments of God in the world—called to preserve it and to bring light into the midst of darkness. To say that we are God's agents for change in our world may sound a bit presumptuous to us, but it is in keeping with Jesus' teaching.

Paul the apostle likewise affirmed those that aspired to leadership when he wrote, "Here is a trustworthy saying: If anyone sets his heart on being an overseer, he desires a noble task" (1 Timothy 3:1). In his commentary on the Pastoral Epistles, Gordon Fee translates this passage: "This is a true saying: If a man is *eager* to be a church leader, he desires an excellent work" (emphasis mine).[9]

Paul's point is not that leadership *per se* is to be desired, but that Christian leadership is an excellent aspiration. Carried into the large context of our world, it would seem true to the text to say, "If someone aspires to offer Christian leadership, they desire an excellent work."

Commenting on that same text, J. Oswald Sanders gives us perspective on the costs of aspiring to be a leader: "To assume this office [in Timothy's time] in the church was to invite persecution, hardship, and even death—even as it does in some lands today. This would surely tend to prevent applications by insincere candidates."[10]

The bottom line? If we desire to offer Christian leadership, if we desire to fulfill our call as salt and light, as change agents in the world, and if we understand the costs that such leadership will entail, then we are starting to rise to the challenge of following Christ in our times.

WHAT CHOICE WILL WE MAKE?

At LEADERSHIP 88, a conference designed to challenge younger leaders to action, Luis Palau, the great evangelist of Latin America, presented his listeners with the three choices facing those who are challenged with leadership:

- to go forward and succeed,
- to go forward and fail,
- or to stay safe and be mediocre.[11]

Going forward involves the risk of success versus failure, but safety is only found in mediocrity. Which will we choose? Gordon MacDonald writes in *Re-Discovering Yourself*, "Will we settle for ordinariness or averageness (as many others seem to be doing), or will we continue the challenge to make sure that something we have done or are doing makes its mark upon our world?"[12]

Mediocrity is the easiest option because it demands nothing of us. Kent Hughes highlights the mediocrity option in *Liberating Ministry from the Success Syndrome.* In it, he cites a letter from a pastor friend who was commenting on what he thought was a swing toward mediocrity in Christian leadership:

> It seems that in trying to correct some possible pastoral abuses of the past, seminaries are exposing their students to a recurring theme: "don't burn out...be sure to get your day(s) off...marriage first, ministry second." These refrains may all be quite true, but they come with such repetitive force that I fear the pendulum has swung from those who jeopardized their families in the name of "ministry" to men who think that they have something coming to them because they are "in the ministry." We now have men who are so thoroughly warned of sacrificing their families that they sacrifice nothing![13]

The people of Hebrews 11, the "Hall of Fame" of faith, were anything but mediocre. In those verses, we read of men and women of faith who—though many of them failed on occasion—by faith conquered kingdoms, fulfilled God's promises, escaped death (or died) for their faith, defeated armies, and killed giants.

May God give us the grace to act on faith so that an updated version of Hebrews 11 can be written of the leaders who bring the Church into the twenty-first century. Men and women who—despite failings and blunders—will by faith address complex ethical issues, complete the Commission to take the gospel to all peoples, act justly in a materialistic world, and build the Kingdom of Christ!

To rise to the challenge of being a leader is a lifelong commitment, but my prayer is that this book will be an encouragement to others (and to myself, as I am also in the learning-to-lead process) to start making choices based on a sense of understanding of our calling to be God's change agents in our world.

The world needs leaders—
who cannot be bought;
whose word is their promise;
who put character above wealth;
who possess opinions and a will;
who are larger than their vocations;
who do not hesitate to take chances;
who will not lose their individuality in a crowd;
who will be honest in small things as well as in great things;
who will make no compromise with wrong;
whose ambitions are not confined to their own selfish desires;
who will not say they do it "because everybody else does it";

who are true to their friends through good report and evil report, in adversity as well as in prosperity;
who do not believe that shrewdness, cunning, and hardheadedness are the best qualities for winning success;
who are not ashamed or afraid to stand for the truth when it is unpopular;
who can say no with emphasis, although the rest of the world says yes.[14]

Part One

The Marks of a Leader

Overwhelmed. This is the feeling that I have in a host of ministry settings. To walk the streets of Haiti or the barrios of Colombia; to hear the stories of atrocities in war-torn Mozambique or injustice in apartheid South Africa; to see people suffering the effects of terrible choices or the disillusionment of unfulfilled dreams—all of these scenarios leave me feeling overwhelmed. What can this one person possibly do in response?

World hunger, poverty affecting two-thirds of our earth, people unreached with the gospel, natural and man-made disasters that threaten or take the lives of thousands, even millions—need I go on to make you feel overwhelmed along with me?

People who aspire to leadership in our world can soon become discouraged when they look at the magnitude of the needs. How do we respond in the face of materialism and secularism? And how can we help in a Christian church that seems at times too fragmented or too irrelevant to be the answer to the hungry, hopeless, and hurting of our world?

All of these problems provide enough challenges to overwhelm us for a lifetime, but they are *not* the greatest challenges facing those who aspire to leadership. They are largely external to us, challenges to which God will call us to respond. However, His first calling on us is internal—dealing with our own growth toward Christlikeness.

Paul the apostle, when writing to exhort his younger counterpart Timothy about leadership, did not focus on the external challenges of the Roman empire of that day. He made mention of religious trends, persecutions, and a variety of other externals that could have overwhelmed young Timothy, but his specific exhortation to Timothy as a young man in leadership focused on Timothy's character. He was giving Timothy a sense of priority: *Develop your character so you can have the inner resources and resolve to lead—no matter what external challenges arise!* He wrote to Timothy:

> Don't let anyone look down on you because you are young, but set an example for the believers in speech, in life, in love, in faith and in purity. (1 Timothy 4:12)

The Greek word translated "example" is the word *tupos*, from which we get *type*. The call to Timothy is to be a "type," a pattern or model of Christlikeness that others can follow. Paul was challenging Timothy to grow in character so that he could exhort others as Paul had—"Follow my example, as I follow the example of Christ" (1 Corinthians 11:1).

THE GREATEST CHALLENGE—TO BE AN EXAMPLE

A few days after Carl had finished his ordination council, I was reviewing his performance with another council member. As we discussed Carl's presentation, I was critical of his seeming inability to quote the Scriptures from memory. When looking for a reason for this lack, I accused the seminary, and I blamed the campus organization he had been involved with in college. My fellow reviewer listened calmly, and then replied, "But Paul, whose ministry has Carl been under for these past three years?"

My accusations were silenced. Carl had been *my* protégé in ministry. If he seemed weak in his ability to accurately handle the Scriptures, who was to blame? All the fingers were now pointing at me. *I* had not been an example of Scripture memory. *I* had not been thorough in leading him by the example of my own life. His performance at that council was a reflection on the person he had modeled himself after—me.

The greatest sermon any leader can preach is their life. Paul exhorts Timothy to pay attention to his life—his example—first. We are the "types" or "patterns" that others are looking to follow. And, as John Stott reminds us, "We preachers cannot expect to communicate from the pulpit if visually out of it we contradict ourselves."[1]

The root of *example* in the Greek language (*tupos*) denotes a blow. In other contexts, *tupos* means an "impression" or the "mark of a blow." In John 20:25, Thomas asks to see the "marks" where the nails were in Jesus' hands. The meaning expands to our personal lives to indicate the mark or impression we can make in an ethical sense through our lives.

We could apply the meaning doubly to our lives. In one sense, we should be examples whose lives are marked or imprinted with the character of Christ. In another sense, we should realize that the greatest imprint we can make on the lives of others is through our model, our example.

Paul's challenge to Timothy was to lead by example. In spite of his inexperience, the difficulties related to his church setting, and his physical weaknesses and nervous temperament, Paul commands him to lead the believers by his lifestyle and godly behavior. The same challenge is ours!

OUR EXAMPLES ARE CRUCIAL

Exemplary leadership demands that we evaluate our lifestyles, attitudes, and modeling before others. Nothing is more revealing than to close the day with an evaluation: "What kind of example have I been today to others?" As in my review of Carl's ordination council, we may find that our example needs repair.

Our Examples Give Our Ministry Credibility

Timothy was a leader whose abilities, age, and theology would have put him under great pressure. Paul does not call him to defensiveness but to exemplary leadership.

Commenting on the passage in 1 Timothy 4:12, Ajith Fernando writes, "The way to silence criticism and to win confidence is by earning respect through an exemplary life." Fernando continues, "Timothy's reputation was at stake. The way to overcome the problem was not a powerful public relations drive, which leaders today are prone to try, but by an exemplary life. *When we take care of our character, our reputation takes care of itself*" (emphasis mine).[2]

I developed the habit of writing in a journal while I was in college. In each spiral notebook "volume," I would write a final page dedicating that edition to someone who had affected me during that time period. In one volume, I made special note of several key figures in my life that year. One had led me in ministry experiences, and another had taught me about preaching. But I had no hesitation in dedicating that volume to the third—a man distinguished by the fact that he had "taught me how to live." His effect on my life was superior because he had exemplified the life he was challenging me to live.

Dr. Tony Campolo distinguishes between power as a leader and authority as a leader. *Power*, he says, is the ability to make others do your will even if they would choose not to. *Authority* is the ability to get others to do what you want because they recognize, through your life and words, that what you ask is legitimate and right.[3] Pilate had power; Jesus had authority. Autocrats and dictators have power, but exemplary leaders have authority.

Our Examples Are Our Most Potent Teaching Tools

The Scriptures are full of exhortations related to teaching by modeling:

- Jesus told His disciples that "everyone who is fully trained will be like his teacher" (Luke 6:40).
- Paul exhorts the Philippians with his own example, telling them to put into practice the things they had "learned or received or heard from me, or seen in me" (Philippians 4:9).
- Paul, as Timothy's teacher, reminds him that he knows "all about my teaching, my way of life, my purpose, faith, patience, love, endurance" and more (2 Timothy 3:10).
- Jesus called men to the life of discipleship with the invitation to "Follow me" (Matthew 4:19).

Too often I am inclined to forget this truth. I think that a new style of communication, a more effective development of my personality, or a greater ability to touch hundreds of lives will enable me to be a better leader. In fact, my example is my greatest teaching tool.

In the book *Soul Friend*, Kenneth Leech tells a story of a dialogue between two monks:

> A brother asked Abba Poemen, "Some brothers live with me; do you want me to be in charge of them?" The old man said to him, "No; just work first and foremost, and if they want to live like you, they will

> see to it themselves." The brother said to him, "But it is they themselves, father, who want me to be in charge of them." The old man said to him, *"No, be their example, not their legislator"* (emphasis mine).[4]

Our most significant impact on others will be through lives well-lived under the lordship of Jesus Christ.

Our Examples Reflect Our Character

Bill Hybels completed a book under the title *Who You Are When No One's Looking*. Ted Engstrom has written a book entitled simply *Integrity*, and Charles Swindoll has written one entitled *The Quest for Character*. These titles reflect a heightened awareness in the Christian community for Christian leaders to consider their personal lives *before* they lead.

Hybels book has the most convicting title because it asks us to consider whether our personal lives match our leadership image. It speaks to our life example.

Anyone who has ever taught or attempted to lead others knows the tendency in all of us toward exaggerating our depth of character while treating leniently our flaws. The Bible calls this tendency *hypocrisy*. We consciously or subconsciously put forward a better image of ourselves than really exists. The outward appearance of our character and the inner reality (that only God, we, and perhaps our family members know) do not match.

C.S. Lewis explains the conflict in *The Four Loves*:

> Those like myself, whose imagination far exceeds their obedience, are subject to a just penalty; we easily imagine conditions far higher than any we have really reached. If we describe what we have imagined we may make others, and make ourselves, believe that we have really been there.[5]

Concentrating on the inner life of the leader speaks to the problem succinctly. Our life example is the greatest reflection of the extent of our sanctification, our likeness to Christ. As we consider the challenge of exemplary leadership in this book, we will realize that growth requires us to face the truth about ourselves and our character, without distortion—no matter how painful such a confrontation might be. We must be willing to undergo self-criticism that will bring our inner character and our outer image into closer alignment.

When the person we are "when no one's looking" is the same as the person that followers, parishioners, or students see leading them, we have demonstrated the desirable quality called integrity. Every Christian leader will spend a lifetime working toward this quality.

One of the unusual privileges I had in the preparation of this book was a discussion with J. Oswald Sanders—missionary statesman, author, Christian leader. At eighty-five years old, he was a vault of wisdom. I asked him what he thought were the greatest words of exhortation he could give to me and others who aspire to leadership. Without hesitation, he responded, *"Watch your devotional life. A Spirit-blessed ministry is founded on a solid devotional life."*[6]

The inner character of the leader is the foundation for effective ministry.

Our Examples Reflect Our Willingness to Serve

Dr. Leighton Ford challenged young men and women to leadership over several years, and one of his themes has been to stir young people to be "Kingdom-seekers," not "empire-builders."[7] He has seen the damage done by those who have sought their own ends rather than God's, and he is now exhorting them to be servants of the Master *first*, so that all know that they are seeking His Kingdom.

To lead by example is to lead by serving. Paul the apostle demonstrated this to the Thessalonians when he resumed his tentmaking vocation to keep from taxing the resources of that church:

> Surely you remember, brothers, our toil and hardship; we worked night and day in order not to be a burden to anyone while we preached the gospel of God to you. (1 Thessalonians 2:9)

> For you yourselves know how you ought to follow our example. We were not idle when we were with you, nor did we eat anyone's food without paying for it. On the contrary, we worked night and day,

> laboring and toiling so that we would not be a burden to any of you. (2 Thessalonians 3:7-8)

The "sense of entitlement" referred to earlier has no place in the life of one who leads by example. Rather than a feeling of "I deserve respect because I am a leader," the young leader says, "I am a servant of Jesus Christ; I will lead others with the same foot-washing spirit of my Master."

In *Waking from the American Dream*, Donald McCullough reminds us of our need to be identified with the Lord Jesus rather than with the "can-do" spirit of our age: "The next time you're tempted to believe that all your desires can be met with enough work and prayer and positive thinking, remember Jesus."[8]

This spirit of servanthood, however, does not entitle us to run from leadership responsibilities. Instead, it enables us to lead with humility. A servant spirit will enable us to pour ourselves into others with the hope and dream that their ministries will outshine ours. It will enable us to rejoice to hear that our "children are walking in the truth" (3 John 4).

The spirit of servanthood will enable us to be more like Timothy, who took a consistent, genuine interest in the welfare of others (Philippians 2:20), than like Diotrephes, who loved (and perhaps needed) to be first (3 John 9).

CONCLUSION

In an interview with *Fortune* magazine, Ken Olsen, the Chief Executive Officer of the Digital Equipment Corporation (DEC), reflected on the struggle of being the "boss" in that successful company. "Being boss offers no advantage in getting anything done. Everyone is out to prove the boss is wrong."[9]

By being the head of his corporation, Ken Olsen sets himself up for greater opposition and criticism than if he were content to be a middle manager, lost somewhere on the company flowchart. But leadership demands that we open ourselves to the critiques and opinions of others.

Nowhere is this challenge greater than in the realm of our own personal example. If Ken Olsen is confronted with people who are out to prove that he is wrong, we likewise will be confronted with people who want to disqualify us as leaders because of our age or inexperience.

The solution? We must work on specific aspects of our Christlike example so that we can be the best exemplary leaders possible. Paul gives Timothy, *and us*, five specific areas of life to work on. Let's get started!

> Awake, my soul, and with the sun
> Thy daily stage of duty run;
> Shake off dull sloth, and joyful rise
> To pay the morning sacrifice.[10]

1
What You Say

Glandion Carney was being introduced by a friend, and this set him up to be the object of a humorous story. The introducer told of a supposed interaction between himself and Glandion's five-year-old son.

"Is your daddy a good preacher?" the man asked.

"Oh, yes!" replied the boy.

"Can he preach without notes?" continued the interviewer.

"Certainly," said the boy. "He's so good he can preach without thinking."[1]

I can remember one occasion where I found myself unprepared before a dinner audience; I remember thinking to myself, "I had better start talking until I think of something to say." I was very capable of letting my mouth speak without the participation of my brain!

Humanity's ability to say words without mental involvement—to preach without thinking—led Paul to list speech as one aspect of the exemplary leadership that young Timothy needed. Paul knew that much of Timothy's ministry would be related to personal conversations and public addresses, so he told him to set an example by his speech.

In the Pastoral Letters (1 and 2 Timothy and Titus), there are no fewer than twenty-seven references to the spoken words of leaders—speech, instruction, or preaching. This emphasis reinforces the importance of a leader's healthy caution over the control of the tongue.

Why is this concern so vital in leadership? Jesus reminds us that our language is a reflection of that which fills the heart (see Matthew 12:34-36). Inner anger can be cloaked with sweet smiles or warm hugs, but our inner character will be revealed by hostile words that spurt forth in a moment of pressure or frustration.

I am often mortified to hear the words that arise when I am cut off in traffic or one of my perceived "rights" is violated. Jesus says that these words are a manifestation of my inner being—which is so desperately in need of transformation!

Charles Spurgeon exhorted ministers-in-training in *Lectures to My Students* with these words: "A minister of Christ should have his tongue, and his heart, and his hand agree."[2] The tongue speaks out and the hand reveals the condition of the inner being.

Our language is secondly a reflection of our concern for others. "A fool," the writer of Proverbs asserts, "finds no pleasure in understanding but delights in airing his own opinions" (18:2). If we spend all of our time talking, it shows our contempt for the concerns of others.

I was in a small group of international leaders when I saw the truth of this verse in action. As each person went around the circle introducing himself or herself, we were eager to listen. Mandla Adonisi of Soweto, South Africa, introduced himself. Another member of the group suddenly broke in, anxious to start a discussion about the difficulties in South Africa. In his zeal, however, he never asked Mandla one question. Instead, he proceeded with a twenty minute revelation of his thoughts on South Africa and his recommended solutions to the problems there. We were all embarrassed because the other man was so demonstrably insensitive to Mandla—the only one who truly understood the oppression of apartheid.

Third, our language is a reflection of our theology. We explain our world in ways that reflect what we believe about God. A fool, the Bible says, lives with a worldview that believes, "There is no God" (Psalm 14:1). Herod was struck down by God because in his self-centered theology, he accepted the praise of others who made him out to be a god (Acts 12:22-23); his ego had distorted his view of God.

Job's counselors spoke in ways that reflected their theology. And at the conclusion of the story, they were rebuked by God because they had not "spoken of me what is right" (Job 42:7). What leader does not tremble at the thought of being rebuked by God for not speaking rightly of Him?

I am sure this is why the psalmist prayed, "May the words of my mouth and the meditation of my heart be pleasing in your sight, O LORD, my Rock and my Redeemer" (Psalm 19:14). He desperately wanted to speak rightly of God.

THE POWER OF SPEECH

Anyone who aspires to leadership desires a manner of speech that reflects godliness of inner character and compassion for others. But the place to start in attaining this is our theology. *Our view of who God is* will be the most powerful motivation toward deeper character and greater love for others.

As we are confronted with the challenge of exemplary speech, we should hear God who tells us to "Be still, and know that I am God" (Psalm 46:10). And perhaps we should paraphrase it, "'Keep quiet and learn who I am,' says the Lord" to ensure that our theological starting point is clear.

The book of James contains the strongest exhortations regarding our tongues. In chapter 3, James offers a colorful description of the tongue, making its power analogous to the rudder of a great ship, a consuming fire, a restless evil, and a deadly poison. In short, James is saying this: WARNING: Misuse of the tongue will be hazardous to spiritual health!

POSITIVE POWER

James summarizes his challenge in verse 2 of chapter 3 when he writes, "If anyone is never at fault in what he says, he is a perfect man, able to keep his whole body in check." Control of speech reflects an overall discipline of life, something most significant to those who aspire to be teachers and young leaders because those who teach and lead will be judged more severely than others (James 3:1).

The Power of Intercessory Prayer

When we think of exemplary speech, we usually focus on oral communication to others. However, this overlooks the greatest positive opportunity and responsibility that God gives us as leaders—to bring the concerns and needs of others before God in prayer.

I once visited members of our church's international missions family, and I asked them what message they would like me to convey to the folks at home on their behalf. Without hesitation, the husband responded, "Tell the people at home that we are depending on their prayers."

My missionary friend was reflecting the same viewpoint that Paul the apostle did to the Corinthians. In the face of great opposition and hardship, Paul wrote of his assurance of God's deliverance "as you [the Corinthians] *help us by your prayers*" (2 Corinthians 1:11, emphasis mine).

Through prayer, we see God work to change people, and we see God work to change us. When I have a particular aversion toward a person (an aversion that might be manifested by hostile words), I find that the best way to bring my own speech under the lordship of Christ is to intercede on behalf of that person. Intercession might not change that person, but it might change me.

Quoting Dean Vaughan in an article entitled "The Prayers of a Leader," J. Oswald Sanders writes, "If I wished to humble anyone, I should ask him about his prayers. I know nothing to compare with this topic for its sorrowful self-confessions."[3]

Indeed, if we are honest before God, we will acknowledge that intercessory prayer lacks the priority attention needed. As young leaders, we are more prone to activity and action; the priestly ministry of intercessory prayer will be a difficult discipline to maintain. I have no doubt that I *should* pray, but I must confess that sometimes I wonder if intercessory prayer is indeed the *most* significant thing I can offer to others. Each leader must wrestle with this struggle in his or her priorities and use of time.

Kent Hughes addresses this struggle when he writes, "God's servants must exercise themselves with an athletic like discipline as they pursue God's purposes for their lives. There will be no prayer life without this discipline."[4]

The Power of Affirmation

On cold winter days, our car battery is sometimes too drained to turn the engine over. When this happens, we rely on someone else's car to come alongside ours and provide the "jump" we need to get started. Our car can run fine if it gets the initial energy it needs from another battery.

The jump-start of a car on a cold day provides a picture of the work of encouragement or affirmation.

There are those who are too weak to get going on their own reserves, but if another comes alongside to give a little "jump," the weaker party may easily be able to start up.

Barnabas is the classical biblical character associated with encouragement. Imagine a man so gifted in encouraging others that the apostles themselves renamed him "Son of Encouragement" (Acts 4:36). His ministry of affirmation built up the new convert Saul (Paul) and helped him become the greatest church planter of New Testament times. Barnabas stuck by his quitter cousin John Mark and offered the "jump-start" he needed to become one of the gospel writers.

One of the contributors to the Proverbs writes, "The tongue of the wise brings healing" (12:18). This is the powerful ministry of encouragement toward which we should all aspire—where our words bring healing to hurting people who desperately need a "jump" to see themselves under the mercy of God.

NEGATIVE POWER

The frightening aspect of our speech, as reflected in James 3, is the damage it can do. The words we speak can harm the spirits of others and ourselves. We are wise to treat our tongue as a fire that needs to be controlled and used for good, not evil.

Negative Speech Leaves Deep Scars

My friend Brian has suffered for many years because he grew up in a home where he was never affirmed.

No matter what successes he achieves as an adult, the words of his father—"You're a loser; you'll never amount to anything"—sound so loud that he is unable to hear anything else. The wounds of cruel words go to the depth of his soul.

Gary Smalley and John Trent discuss the effect of parental words such as these in their book *The Blessing*.[5] The impact of negative or positive words from parent to child is so significant that they can set a pattern for a child's life. (And to those parents reading this—do not underestimate the importance of your affirmation and stated love to your children. Your encouragement to them will help you have the greatest possible positive impact on the "in-house" disciples that God has given you.)

Negative Speech Discredits the Gospel

Several years ago, I took a special interest in the Children of God, a cultic group that had splintered off of mainstream Christianity in the early 1970s. I admired their discipline in prayer and Scripture memorization, but I knew that many aspects of their theology and practice were aberrant.

In my zeal to show them wrong, I learned their techniques, strove to outdo their knowledge of Scripture, and specialized on their flaws. The day of confrontation finally came. I was on the streets of Dallas, Texas, when I was approached by a Children of God member. I listened briefly, but then, with my arsenal fully stocked, I attacked.

To my great delight, I "won." The Children of God

disciple retreated from the conversation, and I walked away, smugly content to be a "cult-buster."

Then God broke through. He convicted me with words in my spirit: "Do you think that person will ever respond to the love of the Jesus you just presented?"

I realized that I had won my battle but in the process had discredited the true gospel message. In obedience to the prompting of the Spirit, I had to relocate my victim and ask his forgiveness for my lack of love.

We do not have to look far these days to see those that have been negatively affected by the speech or behavior of someone who calls himself a Christian. Our inconsistencies of example sometimes lead nonbelievers to reject Jesus.

In the fine book *The Other Side of Leadership*, Eugene Habecker relates a childhood memory of the evangelists who would visit his church. They would come, according to Habecker, with messages that were summed up as follows: "Don't drink, don't smoke, don't dance, save others, witness, prepare for heaven." Habecker observed later in life that one of the strongest advocates of the don't-drink-or-smoke message was an evangelist who weighed more than three hundred pounds.[6] With his mouth decrying one form of bodily abuse and a physique that testified to another, I wonder if his message was heard.

OUR TWO GREATEST FEARS

As I have talked with young leaders about this matter

of exemplary speech, I have found that we have similar fears that fall into two general categories. On one hand, we fear that we will say something stupid; on the other, we fear failing to speak up when it is needed. Let's examine each.

The Fear of Speaking

I do not preach very often, so when I do, I am extremely cautious with my use of illustrations and volatile words. At least I am now—ever since the manure story.

Having worked thirteen years as a youth leader, I had grown accustomed to using graphic illustrations and wild stories to keep students' attention. That's why I thought nothing of it when I compared our lives to manure in a Sunday morning sermon.

When I told the story, some laughed. After the service, a few commented, "That was *quite* an illustration!" But it was two days before I received the letter from Carol.

She told me how she had grown up in a home where she had been constantly told that she was not worth _______ (a synonym for manure). Her conversion had brought her a long way toward healing and a new sense of value.

My sermon, however, had taken her back to the painful memories of her childhood. She asked that I refrain from using the manure story in the future.

She did not need to ask! As I read her letter and thought of the emotional damage I had done, I said to myself, "I should never speak again!" My greatest fears were realized. I had deeply hurt someone with my careless words.

In trying to discipline my tongue, I have memorized a phrase that I ask God to bring to my mind anytime I am teaching or under particular pressure: *Think before you speak!* The words that I shoot out before thinking are the ones I will most likely regret later.

Carole Mayhall writes, "I am convinced that *daily*, perhaps *hourly*, we need to ask God to help us bite our tongue before voicing careless remarks that can hurt, even devastate. We need to ask Him to help us to think before we speak."[7]

The problem with my manure story was my thoughtlessness; I had not considered how my words would be received by my audience. The experience reminded me of James's exhortation to be "slow to speak" (James 1:19). We would all be wise to remember that command every day.

As young leaders, we might also fear speaking past our experience. Jude accuses false prophets of being "clouds without rain" (Jude 12), a vivid picture of one who gives the appearance of character but whose life does not substantiate it. We fear that we will, in the words of the Puritan writer Richard Baxter, "unsay with our lives what we say with our lips."[8]

The best way to overcome our fear of speaking is to make sure that we are listening—to God, to others, and to ourselves. James tells us to be *quick* to listen and *slow* to anger and speech. A popular proverb tells us that with "two ears and one mouth, we ought to be listening twice as much as we speak." Both remind us to listen and think before speaking.

Fear of Staying Silent

Two years ago, Josie committed suicide. She had graduated from high school a few years earlier, and I'd had the privilege of performing her marriage a year before she died. In her first year of marriage, she became very depressed. I visited her in the psychiatric ward of the hospital, where I attempted to offer a few words of counsel and comfort. However, the words seemed empty. Two weeks later she was dead.

When I heard the news about Josie, my first thoughts were of regret: *if only* I had said the right words when I visited her.

On another occasion, I was sitting at the airport, waiting to pick up Mike and Donna, a young missionary couple returning from the mission field after only three months of a four-year term. Their marriage was in deep trouble, and we were bringing them home with the hope of offering the support and counsel that would keep them together.

Surprisingly, I was not shocked that they were returning home. Several of us had seen warning signs of problems in their relationship earlier, but no one spoke up. After all, these were our stars, our "home-grown missionaries." I suppose it was pride that kept us silent. Now I sat in the airport thinking, "*If only* I had spoken when I had the chance—before this problem blew up, embarrassing Mike, Donna, and all involved."

If only are two of the saddest words in our

vocabulary. They reflect the regret of bad decisions or, in my case, of words not spoken at the right time or in the right way.

Courageous words—whether of comfort, confrontation, or encouragement—require us to take risks. Witnessing to non-Christian friends might lead to their rejection of the gospel or us. Confronting a stumbling brother might make him angry or accusatory toward us. But neither risk should keep us silent.

Whether we speak up or stay silent, we are taking risks. But risk-taking is basic to leadership. Our best strategy is to work toward speech that is under God's control.

QUALITIES OF EXEMPLARY SPEECH

The lifelong discipline of bringing our tongue under the Spirit's control starts now. Leadership, according to Paul's command to Timothy, starts by setting an example to the faithful in speech. Consider seven biblical qualities that should mark our speech as leaders.

Affirmation

Thomas Carlyle said, "Tell a man he is brave and you help him become so."[9] Affirmation is powerful speech; it builds others up; it helps them see themselves with greater potential and promise.

The staff of Youth Alive in Soweto, South Africa, asked me to speak to a gathering of 150 young people on a familiar youth ministry topic—self-image (or self-esteem). Unlike the teens I was accustomed to, however, I addressed black township youth who lived under the oppression of apartheid. The world they lived in constantly told them that they were worthless, that they were, in effect, nonpersons.

I knew that I needed to start with affirmation, but not the shallow cheerleading words that told them that they were "special." I had to turn to the Scriptures and affirm them with God's words: that in spite of the explicit and implicit messages of their government, they were precious and loved by a God who endured human oppression for them in the person of Jesus Christ. True affirmation, I learned, is helping people see themselves as recipients of the love of Jesus Christ.

Affirmation builds up others, but it also can change us. When we concentrate on helping others see themselves under the love of Jesus, we change our view of them too.

One of our young men in the Christian education department used to drive me crazy. Every Sunday he would badger me with questions and offer all sorts of advice. After I grew past my initial irritation, I began to see him as an insecure guy who desperately needed attention. Each Sunday I looked for ways to encourage and affirm him. I even grew to the point where I could thank him for his advice! As I verbally affirmed him as a person loved by Jesus, I found that I grew to love him too.

In his book *Rebuilding Your Broken World*, Gordon MacDonald highlights the great need of "broken-world" people for affirmation and encouragement. He calls this the "gift of restorative grace." He writes,

> I can hardly think of a more important function than the giving of grace: to the man or woman who has never learned of the love of Christ and His reclaiming grace. To the young or struggling believer who seeks a Christlike faith and the joy of experiencing reforming grace. And to the broken-world person who has so disappointed his brothers and sisters in faith and needs restorative grace. Where there is grace, there is hope, hope for a broken world to be rebuilt.[10]

Truth / Conviction

I watched a political debate recently. In the course of two hours of questions and answers, there were hundreds—even thousands—of words spoken, but I wondered if there was much commitment to truth. Every comment was carefully couched in non-inflammatory words designed to please the widest possible audience. There were many words, but there was very little truth or conviction.

Truth-telling begins in our inner being. We must be honest before God about ourselves. If we manage to lie to ourselves (rationalizing sinful behavior, keeping secrets from God or our spouses, deceiving ourselves about our own spirituality), our foundations for truth and conviction are badly shaken.

This is why D. Martyn Lloyd-Jones exhorted his ministerial students that "the most important task [of the preacher] is to prepare himself, not his sermon."[11] Our commitment to truthful examination of our own soul by the Holy Spirit through the Scriptures is our best preparation to teach and lead others.

As Christian leaders, we are also committed to outer truthfulness. Exaggeration, overstating an illustration, or minimizing our own sinfulness all serve to discredit us as witnesses. John Stott says,

> It is so easy to exaggerate, to give others the impression that we have progressed further along the narrow way than we really have. We must have the honesty to confess the truth. We should not be afraid to say with the apostle, "not as though I had already attained, either were already perfect."[12]

Truthfulness with ourselves and in our speech enables us to speak with conviction. Our words have a ring of authority when they come from a heart purged by honest self-evaluation.

To assist in the evaluation of our commitment to truthfulness and affirmation, Ted Engstrom offers four penetrating questions in *Seizing the Torch*:

1. Is it the truth?
2. Is it fair to all concerned?
3. Will it build goodwill and better friendships?
4. Will it be beneficial to all concerned?[13]

Compassion

Truthfulness does not give us license to be insensitive to others. Words can be ruthlessly truthful, but if they are spoken without sensitivity to the listener, they can destroy. A "timely word" is a delight (Proverbs 15:23).

A timely word is a compassionate word. A compassionate word is spoken with a full awareness of the pain in the person who listens.

In the course of the preparation of this book, my mother-in-law had been seriously ill. Of the many traumas, perhaps the most serious was the amputation of her left leg.

After the amputation surgery, my father-in-law and I were sitting in the hospital lobby awaiting a report from the doctor. A woman sat by us and engaged us in conversation. As she heard of the difficulties of the past days and the amputation surgery, she responded by telling us of her own mother's leg amputation. "Since that amputation," she said, "my mother has sat in her wheelchair dejected, refusing to eat. She just sits around, hoping to die."

Her insensitivity to the situation astonished me. She left after she realized that she had said something wrong, but her lack of compassion left a lasting impression on my father-in-law. He was emotionally jolted into imagining the worst for his wife's future.

Listening to the insensitive words of this anonymous woman, I remembered the psalmist's commitment of Psalm 39:1 (NASB): "I will guard my mouth as with a muzzle." I asked God to temper my truthfulness with compassion for others, that my words might give grace to those who hear.

CONFRONTATION

Exemplary speech is a complicated balance because our commitment to caring for people (with compassion and affirmation) must be balanced with our commitment to the truth. This combination means we must care enough about people to confront them when they err. The writer of Proverbs tells us, "Faithful are the wounds of a friend" (27:6, RSV).

Mr. and Mrs. Davis felt called in their pre-retirement years to the foreign mission field. They had a deep emotional commitment to go wherever God wanted, but the practical details were not in line. Finances, their family situation, and the realities of the world into which they hoped to go did not seem to confirm this call.

They came to me to share their sense of calling. After listening awhile, I asked, "What do your Christian friends think about this decision?" They responded excitedly, "Oh, they are all one hundred percent behind us; we have received nothing but encouragement from others."

I knew something was amiss because two of the Davis's friends had come to me very concerned about this missions decision. These friends asked me, "Would you please talk them out of it?"

But to their faces these friends were giving encouragement and affirmation concerning the mission calling. I knew then that I was facing a twofold confrontation.

First, I had to confront Mr. and Mrs. Davis with some of the realities of their situation. They came into my office excited about their call to missionary service; they left an hour later wondering about the five or six hard questions I had confronted them with. Eventually, a confrontation with the truth about themselves enabled them to decide that they were not called—at least for now—to foreign missionary service.

Then I had to confront their friends—for to affirm the Davis's call to their faces and then come to ask me to "talk them out of it" was dishonest. I had to confront the inconsistency.

Leadership is uncomfortable. Any man or woman who is too timid to tell people the truth—even when it is hard for them to hear—will have a difficult time leading. The function of a biblical preacher has been described as "comforting the disturbed [compassion] and disturbing the comfortable [confrontation]."[14] The former may win us many friends, but the latter may lead us to loneliness.

Bill Hybels addresses confrontation in the book *Who You Are When No One's Looking* under the designation "Tough Love." He states that there are two fundamental convictions that provide the foundation for confrontation: "First, he or she must believe that *truth telling is more important than peace keeping.* Second, he or she must realize that *the well-being of the other person is more important than the current comfort level in the relationship....* Peace at any price is a form of deception from the pit of hell." And he concludes, "A relationship built on peace keeping won't last. Tough love chooses truth telling over peace keeping and trusts God for the outcome."[15]

Forgiveness / Reconciliation

Godly speech ministers grace to the listener. The book of Proverbs affirms that "the tongue that brings healing is a tree of life" (15:4). The greatest words we can ever offer someone else are through the restatement of the gospel to them personally: "Through Jesus, *your* sins are forgiven; you are accepted."

Ministering forgiveness to others starts with a personal understanding of our own sinfulness and the grace that God has given to forgive us. An acute awareness that we are "wounded healers" is a prerequisite to helping others experience God's grace. The faithful leader, therefore, must learn early of his or her own sinfulness and, when needed, to ask the forgiveness of others.

Some of my most humbling experiences in ministry have occurred when I realized that my sinful attitudes or speech had hurt others and I needed—privately or publicly—to ask others to forgive me. These experiences of humiliation, however, have been used by God to help others ask forgiveness of people that they had offended. Leaders will not lead people further than they themselves are willing to go, and the best teacher of relational reconciliation is personal example.

The leader must also minister grace to others by affirming to the guilt-ridden that the grace of Christ is sufficient. In a sense, every Christian leader can be the agent through which forgiveness is experienced by the broken. While the Roman Catholic practice of priests granting the forgiveness of God is unbiblical, the practice of verbally stating to others that God, in Christ, forgives them should be part of a healing ministry.

Perhaps the most difficult aspect of the ministry of reconciliation entrusted to leaders is the hard work required to put separated people back together with each other. The "peace at any price" style (referred to earlier) may lead us to ignore it when two Christians are at odds with each other, but a commitment to the ministry of forgiveness will call us to confront these two in an effort to allow them to realize the forgiveness of Christ in their relationship to each other.

Wisdom

Every young leader should emulate Solomon by asking for wisdom, for we need the ability to distinguish between right and wrong. Leadership teaches us to ask, with Solomon, "For who is able to govern this great people of yours?" (1 Kings 3:9).

Wisdom is applied knowledge, the ability to discern, interpret, and understand life. Through education and literature, we live in an era in which there is no shortage of knowledge, but there is a critical need for wisdom.

The biblical sense of wisdom pertains to our ability to apply the Word of God to daily living. Another term for this is *relevance*. Effectiveness in teaching and leading others correlates directly with our ability to help them see the relevance and application of

Scripture to their lives.

Wisdom also pertains to our ability to remain silent when necessary. Proverbs instructs us that "even a fool is thought wise if he keeps silent" (17:28). I saw Jim ignore this principle as he counseled a young woman who was distraught about the condition of her unsaved family members. Rather than listening compassionately, Jim wanted to give the *right* answer. He replied, "Well, when I got serious about praying for my family, they all became Christians."

The young woman was crushed. She had been praying for her family for ten years. Now Jim seemed to be telling her that something was wrong with her prayers. She walked away demolished.

Jim would have been wiser to keep silent. A compassionate ear was nullified by an overzealous mouth.

Carole Mayhall writes a prayer of sorts in *Words that Hurt, Words that Heal*: "Please then, deliver me from clichés. Deliver me from pat answers. Deliver me from surface statements about complex issues. Deliver me from careless speech."[16] We might add a conclusion: "Oh, Lord, make me wise."

HUMOR

J. Oswald Sanders, in his classic work *Spiritual Leadership*, lists a sense of humor as a quality essential to leadership. He cites A.E. Norrish, a missionary to India, as stating, "I have never met leadership without a sense of humor; this ability to stand outside oneself and one's circumstances, to see things in perspective and laugh. It's a great safety valve! You will never lead others far without the joy of the Lord and its concomitant, a sense of humour."[17]

One of the temptations that overtakes young leaders is the tendency to take themselves far too seriously—as if they were the key link in the chain of God's activities on earth. A dour spirit and an exaggerated commitment to seriousness can be oppressive to listeners and followers.

In leadership, we must learn the difference between taking life or ministry seriously and taking ourselves seriously. The realities of life and death, Heaven and hell, and salvation versus lostness are never laughing matters, but the amazing fact that God uses frail human beings like us in the process is often hilarious. We should never have such an inflated view of our abilities or our call from God that we forget to laugh at ourselves.

Several years ago, I was invited to a very significant conference for young leaders. The invitation fed my pride; I was tempted to think myself important—until God allowed me to find out that my selection was based on my geographic location, not my leadership potential. When I learned from a member of the selection committee the reason I had been invited—"Because you were the only one from New England who applied;" I was properly humbled. Later my wife and I laughed at my own presumptuousness. She added to the humor by telling me that the information was God's way of making sure that I did not become "a legend in my own *mind*."

Humor tempers our speech with laughter and joy.

The critical issue is timing. A joke in one context may keep a listening audience stimulated and involved in the message. In another context, humor could be totally inappropriate and could detract from the good word spoken. The *Latin America Evangelist* wrote of Kenneth Strachan: "He had a keen sense of humor, but he had a sense of the fitness of things. He knew the place for a joke and his humor was controlled."[18]

CONCLUSION

Will we preach without thinking or talk until we think of something to say? Every leader wrestles with his or her speech because so much of our leadership has to do with verbal communication.

Paul summed up the challenge of exemplary speech in his words to the Ephesian believers: "Do not let any unwholesome talk come out of your mouths, but only what is helpful for building others up according to their needs, that it may benefit those who listen" (Ephesians 4:29).

2
What You Do

The life of a Christian leader has been likened to life in a fishbowl; everybody can watch you, and there is no place to hide. Various experiences have reinforced the reality of the fishbowl life to me, but two stand out.

The first occurred after my wife and I escaped church responsibilities for ten days at the Cinnamon Bay Campground on St. John in the U.S. Virgin Islands. We had been planning this vacation for almost two years, and we were excited to be able to flee the cares of ministerial life for a short period.

The day we arrived on St. John, we were walking through the tiny capital of Cruz Bay. A woman on the street looked at us and did a doubletake. She inquired, "Grace Chapel?" We said yes, introduced ourselves, and found that she and her husband had a retirement home on the island. They were members of our church, and she invited us over for a visit.

The encounter on St. John was largely a pleasant one, but it made us realize that we can never "let down" our standards of Christian living. We could have easily thought to ourselves, "Well, we are almost 3,000 miles from home on an island of less than 3,000 people. Let's drop our guard and do things we would never do at home."

Seeing this church member reminded us of the biblical mandate that leaders must be above reproach, circumspect about their lives. There is never a time to forget that we are examples.

A second experience occurred right here at home. We have many trees around our house, and as a result, we always seem to be raking and cleaning up. Every Thursday, we put our trash barrels out on the street to be collected.

Our home is on a main road that goes to Grace Chapel. Thus, many parishioners pass our home daily. One Thursday, a church attender stopped by the office, saw me in the hallway, and said, "My husband and I have been wondering for the past several months how you and your wife manage to fill seven barrels of trash *every week.*"

I was amazed that my ability to fill trash cans had been a matter of discussion for several months. I thought about responding defensively by telling the woman that my trash was not her concern, but I remembered that my life as a leader is lived in the fishbowl. God gave me grace, and I satisfied her curiosity by explaining that we had many trees.

The experience brought me back to the realization that as a Christian leader, my life is an open book. People observe it, feel free to criticize it (even my ability to fill trash cans!), and sometimes (by God's grace) imitate it. To be a leader is to live in a fishbowl.

CONDUCT EQUALS LIFESTYLE

The fishbowl reality is uncomfortable, something most of us would like to avoid. But Paul commanded Timothy to show himself to be an example to the believers by his conduct. The way that Timothy lived—his values, behavior, lifestyle—was a key part of his teaching ministry through personal example.

Our manner of living is our greatest example, but it also holds our greatest potential for failure. Whether we fear the revelation of some sinful act from our past or the discovery of some tragic flaw of the present, the thought of having our lives examined by others makes us tremble.

We could look at our conduct, measure it according to the Scriptures, and hand in our resignation as leaders. When we see the failures of our own lives, we are prone to disqualify ourselves because we think that we *cannot* be examples.

Robert Raines's poem of self-confession serves to convict us all with respect to our inconsistent conduct and motives:

I am like James and John
Lord, I size up other people
in terms of what they can do for me;
how they can further my program,
feed my ego,
satisfy my needs,

give me strategic advantage.
I exploit people,
ostensibly for your sake,
but really for my own sake.
Lord, I turn to you
to get the inside track
and obtain special favors,
your direction for my schemes,
your power for my projects,
your sanction for my ambitions,
your blank checks for whatever I want.
I am just like James and John.[1]

We identify with such a poem because we know our own sins—whether of conduct or motivation or leadership. We *are* like James and John, *but this does not disqualify us for leadership!* Look what Jesus did through imperfect people like James and John!

Rather than being a disqualifier for leadership, realizing our frailty is a prerequisite: "How blest are these who *know their need* of God" (Matthew 5:3, NEB, emphasis mine).

We know our need. We, with God, acknowledge that we are dust (Psalm 103:14). In that humble posture, we receive God's grace so that He can make us capable of exemplary conduct and lifestyle. We know that He can do it with us,

- because He required it of Timothy (I Timothy 4:12), and we know that God gives the grace for

His commands to be obeyed;
- because it is exemplified in people like Daniel, who "distinguished himself...by his exceptional qualities" (Daniel 6:3), a reflection of the fact that he determined to live an undefiled lifestyle (Daniel 1:8);
- because Jesus changed the rough characters who made up the apostolic band to the point that they were recognized as "having been with Jesus" (Acts 4:13);
- because He commands us to "walk in a manner worthy" of the gospel (Ephesians 4:1, Philippians 1:27, 1 Thessalonians 2:12).

In our own strength, it is impossible to live in a way that exemplifies Christlike conduct, but as we rely on and trust Jesus, He enables us to do so.

EXEMPLARY CONDUCT NEEDED

There are many ways that we could look at this matter of exemplary conduct, but let's focus on four that are especially challenging to the young leader.

Marriage and Family Life

For the married leader, exemplary conduct starts with spouse and children. For the unmarried leader, the context includes "primary relationships." In either context, we are referring to the people with whom we live and relate most, and the relationships that others are most likely to observe as they examine our lives.

To maintain consistency in these primary relationships is more challenging than pastoring a church of 10,000 people or going on a worldwide crusade. At home, our most unregenerate characteristics somehow come to the surface.

Mark Hatfield, a senator from Oregon and exemplary Christian leader in politics, was interviewed in Harold Myra's book *Leaders.* Commenting on family life, Hatfield said,

> The home is the toughest environment of all for leaders. Why is it that the ones we love most are the ones we are most impatient with? My wife has often said to me, "I wish you were as patient with your children as you are with your constituents." She's right. She reminds me that I'm accountable to God and to my family, and I'm grateful for that.[2]

Exemplary conduct must be relational. In Proverbs 6:16-19 (the "Seven Deadly Sins"), at least four of the things God hates pertain to our relationships with others:

- a lying tongue,
- hands that shed innocent blood,
- a false witness who pours out lies,
- one who stirs up dissension among brothers.

The other three (haughty eyes, hearts that devise wicked schemes, and feet that rush to evil) could probably manifest themselves in relationships too. The point is this: in our efforts to set forth an exemplary lifestyle, *we must be cautious to maintain healthy relationships*. God cares about our relationships.

As young leaders, we may want to sacrifice family or marriage for success. We may rationalize, "Just a little more work, and I will achieve my full potential; I will attend to my spouse and family *later*." Tragically, the Christian road is scattered with high-potential leaders who fell by the wayside in their thirties or forties because they failed to give proper priority to their marriage and family. When our primary relationships break apart, our ability to set an example by godly conduct loses credibility.

I am pleased to report, however, that developing healthy marriage and family relationships is possible. When my wife and I were first married, we prayed that God would use our marriage as a testimony of His love. Almost ten years after we were married, one of our single friends paid us a high compliment. She told us that our relationship was one of the best advertisements for marriage she had seen. Christie and I were thrilled to have our lives be examples through a healthy, loving marriage! We thanked God for answering our prayers.

INTEGRITY

James exhorts every Christian to be a doer of the Word, not merely a hearer who deceives himself (James 1:22). Integrity in lifestyle is summed up in that verse: that we try to live the Christian life *before* we teach it.

I once worked in a warehouse unloading fruit and produce from trucks and trains. My boss was a long-term veteran of the business, and on my second day of work he told me, "Paul, I will never ask you to do something that I cannot do better and faster than you." At first I thought he was being haughty, but over the next few months I learned that he was demonstrating integrity. He refused to live in a way that said, "Do as I say, not as I do."

Exemplary conduct flows from a life of integrity, but such conduct is a rigorous discipline for leaders because we are aware of our own inconsistencies. Ted Engstrom writes in *Integrity* that it is "dishonest to preach on the value of a quiet time when you've never done it yourself. It's dishonest to talk about the power of prayer and lead a prayerless life. Isn't it dishonest to talk about forgiveness and fail to forgive?"[3]

Charles Spurgeon exhorted his students that a minister should take care "that his personal character agrees in all respects with his ministry." He went on to illustrate his point by telling the story of "a man that preached so well and lived so badly, that when he was in the pulpit everybody said he ought never to come out again, and when he was out of it they all declared he ought never to enter it again."[4]

Spurgeon presented an exaggerated picture of one who lacked integrity, but we can all identify areas of our own lives where our conduct and ministry do not agree.

The issue of integrity addresses another aspect of our endeavors toward exemplary living— it speaks to the quality of humility. Integrity in leadership implies that we are humble enough to lead without getting consumed with power or prestige.

Paul Tournier warns that "ambition and violence increase inexorably with power."[5] The leader who pursues power easily rationalizes away a lack of integrity or inconsistency of life because the end—*control*—justifies living at a level different from that expected of followers. John Stott writes that "power is safe only in the hands of those who humble themselves to serve."[6]

Bill Hybels related a story of integrity in *Leadership Magazine*. It illustrates proper humility in a leader.

> One evening I stopped by the church just to encourage those who were there rehearsing for the spring musical. I didn't intend to stay long, so I parked my car next to the entrance. After a few minutes, I ran back to my car and drove home.
>
> The next morning I found a note in my office mailbox. It read: *A small thing, but Tuesday night when you came to rehearsal, you parked in the "No Parking" area. A reaction from one of my crew (who did not recognize you after you got out of your car) was, "There's another jerk in the 'No Parking' area!" We try hard not to allow people—even workers—to park anywhere other than the parking lots. I would appreciate your*

> *cooperation, too.* It was signed by a member of our maintenance staff.
>
> [This man's] stock went up in my book because he had the courage to write to me about what could have been a slippage in my character.
>
> And he was right on the mark. As I drove up that night, I had thought, I shouldn't park here, but after all, I am the pastor. That translates: "I'm an exception to the rules." But that employee wouldn't allow me to sneak down the road labeled "I'm an exception."
>
> I'm not the exception to church rules or any of God's rules. As a leader, I am not an exception; I'm to be the example. According to Scripture, I am to live in such a way that I can say, "Follow me. Park where I park. Live as I live."[7]

Hybels has integrity; there is no room for abusing leadership power by declaring oneself an exception to the rules. Exemplary conduct means encouraging others to imitate us, even in the small matters.

Integrity manifests itself in one other way: in our commitment to pray. As young leaders, we might depend on energy and enthusiasm (a resource we'll discuss later in this book) at the expense of prayer and dependence on God. However, if we understand the call to lead an exemplary life, we will understand that *we must pray.* Energy and enthusiasm cannot change us so that our ministries and our lives agree. We are dependent on God to do the sanctifying work of the Holy Spirit, and we draw on that power in prayer.

ATTITUDES

Our ability to lead others and to model proper Christian conduct will be strongly affected by the attitudes we choose. We do not necessarily choose our life situations, but God does allow us to choose our attitudes in response to them. "Events give us pain or joy," wrote Paul Tournier, "but our growth is determined by our personal response to both, by our inner attitude."[8]

Viktor Frankl became a famous psychiatrist through his studies of fellow prisoners in a Nazi concentration camp during World War II. He studied why some died and others survived, and he arrived at one basic theme: *attitude*. He wrote of those that walked through the concentration camp huts "comforting others, giving away their last piece of bread. They may have been few in number, but they offer proof that everything can be taken from a man but one thing: the last of the human freedoms—to choose one's attitudes in any given set of circumstances."[9]

While meeting multiple personal challenges this past year, my attitudes were becoming negative and filled with self-pity. After reading about Frankl, I discovered that my life was degenerating because I was choosing bad attitudes in response to circumstances out of my control. I set a disciplinary goal according to the acrostic S-W-E-A-T. I knew I needed discipline in:

Scripture study,
Writing (the discipline of writing in my journal),
Exercise (bodily discipline),
Attitudes (working to choose godly responses to difficult circumstances), and
Time (living by godly priorities and disciplined use of time).

It may seem unusual to list attitude as a discipline, but I believe it is. The book title *Happiness Is a Choice* summarizes the discipline well. We can choose our attitudes, and the attitudes that we choose affect us, our outlook on the future, and our ability to lead others.

A friend of mine is incredibly effective in his ability to train others to do evangelism, and I would point to one factor: He conveys an attitude of expectancy, and his attitude is contagious.

Attitudes that we choose also affect our perspectives toward others. If we choose an attitude of self-pity, we can easily imagine that no one else cares for us. If we choose an attitude of servanthood, we may feel more loved than ever before.

A godly example in our conduct implies that we are making godly choices in our responses to the hardships and challenges of life. Like Paul in prison, we can choose to "rejoice in the Lord" and "be content whatever the circumstance" (Philippians 4:4,11). Attitude is a disciplinary choice.

Leadership

The Apostle Paul told Timothy that setting an

example in conduct would manifest itself in Timothy's leadership of the people of Ephesus. In the same way, our example should be reflected in our leadership lifestyle.

The leadership lifestyle means the willingness to stand alone—even in the face of great opposition. Mark Hatfield again illustrates this quality. On one occasion during the Vietnam war, governors (he was then the governor of Oregon) were asked to vote in favor of President Johnson's policy. Hatfield, a known opponent of the war was told "don't rat on America." If he could not vote in favor of the policy, he was asked to be absent from the room during the vote. Hatfield refused, and when the vote was taken, he cast the lone dissenting vote. He risked reputation and political career to stand for what he believed in.[10]

Leadership lifestyle means the courage to speak up, even when it is easier to stay silent. I was sitting in a department store reading the newspaper as my wife shopped. I looked up and observed a young woman across the store taking clothes off the rack and shoving them into her shopping bag. I yelled across the store, "Hey, what are you doing?" She ran, fearful of the penalties of shoplifting, but she was apprehended. After I had spoken up, I realized I was now involved. The woman—or her big, bad boyfriend—could now target me for revenge.

Leadership lifestyle means being willing to accept responsibility for our choices. Hudson Taylor walked Brighton Beach in England, contemplating the fact that he was recruiting people to go to China with the China

Inland Mission. He knew that many would die there; others would bury their children. He was tempted to let the gravity of the situation overwhelm him, but he did not. He obeyed God and accepted the fact that, from a human vantage point, he would be blamed for the sufferings in the lives of those he recruited.

Leadership lifestyle means commitment to serve. Phil and I were discussing his possible involvement with our youth ministry after seminary when Jack sat down. It turned out that Jack was also recruiting Phil. Jack started the conversation boldly, "Paul, if Phil goes to work at your multiple staff church, he'll be one among many. If he comes with us, we'll make him a *star*!" I thought to myself, "If he wants to be a star, you can have him."

The need of the hour is for leaders who will understand that exemplary conduct means laying down our lives for our brothers and sisters.

THE STRUGGLE TO LIVE "ABOVE REPROACH"

The fishbowl life of leadership is summed up in the biblical command that a leader must be one who is "above reproach" (1 Timothy 3:2) or "blameless" (Titus 1:7). Paul commanded that leaders set such examples in conduct so that they would strive to live lives that were above criticism.

Anyone who has attempted to lead knows the magnitude of this challenge. It is especially true for the young because youth and wisdom do not often go together. Sometimes we learn how difficult it is to be above reproach only after our failures become public information.

Being above reproach can be confused with pleasing everyone. Kent Hughes quotes the humorous description of "The Ideal Pastor" as a testimony of the impossibility of making everyone happy:

> The Ideal Pastor:
> is always casual but never underdressed,
> is warm and friendly but not too familiar,
> is humorous but not funny,
> calls on his members but is never out of the office,
> is an expository preacher but always preaches on the family,
> is profound but comprehensible,
> condemns sin but is always positive,
> has a family of ordinary people who never sin,
> has two eyes, one brown and the other blue![11]

To be above reproach does not mean that everyone likes or approves of everything we do. Instead, it refers to our exemplary conduct. As people examine our life, do they find a man or woman striving after godliness?

To Be Above Reproach Means Making a Personal Commitment to Excellence

If we want to set an example by our lifestyle, it means commitment to grow to our full potential in Christ. (And when we fail, it means we get back up!)

Gary Inrig distinguishes "success" versus "excellence" in his book *A Call to Excellence*. He says that success is being better than everyone else; excellence is being our personal best. In a sense, then, a person could be a success without being excellent—if the success did not demand that the person do his or her best.

"Excellence," Inrig writes, "is the maximum exercise of one's gifts and abilities within the range of responsibilities given by God."[12] And this excellence is measured *first in our character.* Thus, a leader could look eminently successful in ministry and yet be a failure in character.

My father took me to a track meet in Boston Garden when I was seventeen. It was not very exciting, but one event has stuck in my mind ever since that night. It was the run/walk mile—a difficult event that received little attention because of the unusual "wiggle" with which the competitors run.

Other events were occurring simultaneously, so no one paid much attention to the run/walk, that is, until the event was nearly over. In the course of four laps, one of the slower runners had fallen a full lap behind; as others were completing the race, he was just finishing lap number three. Those of us who were watching were embarrassed for him and expected him to sit down. He did not. He kept on going. All the other runners were finished, but he persevered.

Now the run/walk began to attract attention. As he rounded the second turn, people began to clap. As he wiggled around turn number three, the applause intensified. As he finished the final turn and started down the stretch, the fans gave him a standing ovation! The other runners had achieved success, *but this man was applauded for his excellence*! Everyone appreciated an athlete who refused to quit.

Brian Harbour picks up on this theme in *Rising Above the Crowd*: "Success means being *the* best. Excellence means being *your* best. Success, to many, means being better than everyone else. Excellence means being better tomorrow than you were yesterday. Success means exceeding the achievements of other people. Excellence means matching your practice with your potential."[13]

Excellence of character is the mark of exemplary conduct. Character takes precedence over career, ministry, or outward success. Determining this as a priority takes courage—especially if we have achieved outward success.

I admire Sammy Tippit for this type of courage. In spite of ministerial success as a young man (several books published, an international evangelistic ministry founded, and a strategic ministry established in Eastern European countries), he was willing to cut back his visible ministry in order to renew his commitment to Christian growth. "My ministry had grown larger than my character," he wrote in *Fire in Your Heart*. He decided to cut back—to pastor a small, relatively obscure church—so that he could renew his commitment to personal godliness.[14]

Charles Spurgeon spoke to young men in ministry training concerning their commitment to holy character: "Take heed, therefore, to yourselves first, that you be that which you persuade others to be, and believe that which you persuade them daily to believe, and have heartily entertained that Christ and Spirit which you offer unto others."[15]

To Be Above Reproach Means a Commitment to Holiness

In the past, Christians talked freely of their commitment to "separation." In general, this reflected an understanding of the call to live devout lives in a sin-stained world. It was communicated in the phrase, "Others may—but I cannot."

In the spirit of Christian freedom, we do not talk much anymore about separation from our world. I have heard of "Christian" conferences that feature an open bar at the registration center or include off-color humor as part of the conference plenary sessions. In our new found freedom, perhaps the pendulum has swung to the other extreme.

A leader committed to the imitation of Christ must be separate—from the world and even from fellow Christians! Leaders incur a "stricter judgment," according to James. Jesus' words "unto whom much is given is much required" remind us that accountability is increased with responsibility.

Holiness flows from a life dedicated to becoming like Jesus—no matter what the social costs. If holiness is to be reflected in our conduct, we must accept the rigors of spiritual discipline and "separation."

Robert Murray McCheyne wrote to Dan Edwards after the latter's ordination as a missionary, "In great measure, according to the purity and perfections of the instrument, will be the success. It is not great talents God blesses so much as great likeness to Jesus. *A holy minister is an awful weapon in the hand of God*" (emphasis mine).[16]

Holiness means a personal commitment to the grueling process of spiritual growth that will help us develop a "great likeness to Jesus."

EXEMPLARY CONDUCT IS DISCIPLINE

When Paul wrote to the Corinthians about the Christian life, he used the analogies of a running track and a boxing ring (1 Corinthians 9:24-27). The strict training and diligent efforts of the athlete were for one purpose: to win the prize. Paul concluded by reiterating his own commitment to such spiritual discipline so that he could be an effective and qualified leader.

Leading by example calls us to discipline our own lives, even as we live in the plain view (the fishbowl) of others. Our lives—including our speech and conduct—are the most effective teaching tools we have. The challenge before us is to discipline ourselves so that we grow toward Christlike character, conduct, and lifestyle.

Gordon Maxwell devoted himself to such a discipline. He went to India as a missionary, and his Christian conduct and commitment were evident to all. On one occasion, he asked a Hindu man to teach him the local language. The Hindu man replied, "No, sahib, for you will convert me to Christianity."

Maxwell tried to clarify: "You don't understand; all I want you to do is to teach me the language." But the

Hindu man replied, "I will not, for *no one can live with you and not become a Christian*."[17]

That is Christ-like conduct!

3

The Impact of Love

We live in a culture bent on "having it all." "Me-ism" and the "Culture of Narcissism" have become accepted terms to describe the spirit of our age. A beer commercial asks, "Who says you can't have it all?" and a presidential campaign attracts voters by reminding them that they have greater personal wealth now than they did before that administration took office.

The intensification of self-centeredness and selfish satisfaction leads to a loss of love—at least love of the sacrificial nature described in the Bible. Even secular sociologists acknowledge that "our values and priorities have changed. *Helping isn't a national priority anymore*" (emphasis mine).[1]

A society built on Christian morals focuses on doing good; a society built on self-centeredness focuses on doing well. Personal achievement, affluence, and happiness become the goal, and in the process, the willingness to sacrifice for others is lost.

In *Waking from the American Dream*, Donald McCullough notes that the turning from doing good to doing well is a result of our growing affluence and leisure as a culture. Rather than exploring the frontiers of new territories, we now turn inward to a new frontier: ourselves. McCullough writes,

> Concurrent with the social traumas of the sixties and seventies, the human potential movement sent us into a self-improvement orgy of psychological therapy and sensitivity groups, fat farms, and sex camps, Eastern meditation and self-esteem seminars, jogging and golfing, bean sprouts and megavitamins, and so on—journeying further and further into a new and improved *me*.[2]

While he overstates his case, his point is clear: we live in a culture that has turned inward, looking for fulfillment within ourselves. In such a culture, the biblical idea of finding oneself by selflessly serving and loving another will be hard to comprehend. Telling others to lay down their lives in sacrificial love will not win popular approval.

When Paul called Timothy to set an example to the believers "in love," he called him (and us) to countercultural living, especially if we apply it to our contemporary culture. While the culture is turning inward, our attention is outward. While the culture is asking, "How can I have it all?" we are asking, "Where can I best serve?" While the culture is encouraging us to "look out for number one," we concentrate on setting an example of selfless love.

As young leaders—those called out from the "Me Generation"—the challenge is to exemplify a life marked by love.

THE QUALITIES OF LOVE

Biblical love of the selfless variety knows few parallels in the cultural drift mentioned above, for biblical love is marked by servanthood, sacrifice, and even death.

A *servant* exists to make someone else better. Servanthood, therefore, is the quality of devotion to the betterment of others. Good servants do whatever their job requires without question or hesitation. They exist to be obedient to their masters.

Elisabeth Elliot notes, "I believe the church will be more effective in raising up leaders when we begin to teach and exemplify servanthood." She cites Stephen (who served tables) and Moses and David (who tended sheep). She goes on to write,

> People are often doing ordinary things when God calls them to do what turn out to be great things. Jesus said, "If you are willing to be last, then you will be first. If you're willing to do the small things, then I will make you ruler over many things." It's one of those biblical paradoxes where the principle of the Cross goes into operation—you gain by losing; become great by becoming small. When we as the Church evade the Cross we are cutting

> ourselves off from the possibility of true spiritual leadership. And that is the kind of leadership that we need today more than ever.[3]

Sacrifice is a second quality of love. The greatest demonstration of love is to lose or voluntarily sacrifice something for the sake of another person or purpose. "The real qualities of leadership," wrote Sanders, "are to be found in those who are willing to suffer for the sake of objectives great enough to demand their wholehearted obedience."[4]

Sacrifice and suffering go hand in hand, and this adds to the aversion we have to both. We would rather be like the people described in a Charles Williams novel who "liked their religion taken mild."[5]

To love enough to sacrifice may not always mean personal suffering. It may mean the willingness to lay down dreams or aspirations, to back down from a well-formed opinion, to voluntarily lose individual freedoms for the good of others. These sacrifices often cause more pain because they require us to attack our pride.

Death is a third quality of biblical love. The example of Jesus calls us to deny ourselves and take up His cross daily (Luke 9:23). The Apostle John wrote, "This is how we know what love is: Jesus Christ laid down his life for us. *And we ought to lay down our lives for our brothers*" (1 John 3:16, emphasis mine).

At an Urbana missions conference, several of the speakers were interviewed about their commitment to urban ministry. They were asked about the fears they might have entertained regarding the safety of their spouses and children. Ray Bakke, a resident of inner-city Chicago for almost 20 years, answered openly without hesitation: "We must remember: Missionaries have always buried their children on the mission field." Bakke's love honestly confronted the reality of death.

While only a few will be called to literal martyrdom, all of us are called to love others and, in so doing, to die daily. It might mean paying for the opportunity to serve—as many missionaries and pastors often do. It could mean loving that person whom we would run from if it were not for the love of Christ. It will mean considering the needs of others as priorities before our own.

WHAT DOES IT MEAN TO BE AN "EXEMPLARY LOVER"?

As young leaders, we are called to set an example to the believers by our love. In the context of Christian leadership and modeling, what will this mean?

Exemplary Love Gives

The Apostle Paul wrote to the Roman believers, "But God demonstrates his own love for us in this: While we were still sinners, Christ died for us" (Romans 5:8). The example that Jesus set showed us love that is given without reciprocation. We were helpless, but He gave Himself; we had nothing to offer Him.

Giving without reciprocation starts in our worship of God. As Mary sat at the feet of Jesus and so chose "what is better" (Luke 10:38-42), we likewise must commit ourselves to *worship before service.* A.W Tozer wrote, "God wants worshippers before workers,"[6] and we who are young, action-oriented, and restless to get into the battle need to listen. We must give ourselves to worshiping God first.

Abraham, a contemporary from India, sat with my perspective wife Christie and me and described his restlessness over the job God had given him. He talked of monotonous administration, boring phone calls, and the difficulties of dealing with his organization's constituents. He knew, he told us, that God had higher purposes for him. He desired to be a great evangelist and to influence thousands for Christ. Right now, however, he felt boxed in.

Christie commented to me later, "Perhaps God has boxed Abraham in to get his attention so that he desires God first and not greatness as an evangelist." Her observation about Abraham convicted me; I, too, can aspire to fulfill my "sense of destiny" rather than realizing that I am first called to give myself to God without reservation.

A spirit of worship leads us to demonstrate love without reciprocation through intercessory prayer. Prayer provides an avenue of unreciprocated service to others that only God Himself knows about. (See chapter 1, "What You Say," for more on intercession.)

Giving without reciprocation is also a theme for any who aspire to follow the example of Christ. In Christian leadership, we will go through the feelings of being ignored or unappreciated (or undiscovered as our friend

Abraham was feeling), but these feelings should lead us back to self-examination, wherein we recommit ourselves to serving, even if nobody notices.

The spirit of western Christianity militates against the spirit of selfless giving. We exalt men and women at our conferences; we give financial awards for deeds of service done in obscurity; we are sometimes guilty of giving others their "reward in full" in this life. Some are developing attitudes about pastoral ministry that prompts them to ask about the salary package before examining God's call. By asking, "What's in it for me?" they overlook the fact that God calls leaders to suffer while fulfilling the Church's mission.

Amy Carmichael, the founder of the Donhavur Fellowship in India, wrote these words to exhort us all to give without reciprocation in our commitment to follow Christ. Read it slowly:

Hast thou no scar?
No hidden scar on foot, or side, or hand?
I hear thee sung as mighty in the land,
I hear them hail thy bright ascendant star:
Hast thou no scar?

Hast thou no scar?
Yet, I was wounded by the archers, spent,
Lean me against the tree to die, and rent
By ravening beasts that compassed me, I swooned:
Hast thou no wound?

No wound? No scar?
Yes, as the master shall the servant be,

And pierced are the feet that follow Me;
But thine are whole. Can he have followed far
Who has no wound? No scar?[7]

Exemplary Love Serves

Bob is the eldest member of our pastoral staff, and he sets before us an example of humility and service. He spends much of his time caring for the needy, visiting the sick, and counseling the broken. From a human vantage point, his work seems to have few rewards. But Bob does not do it for the rewards. He does it because he is obedient; he does it because he knows that love means serving.

Stuart and Sindia fall into the "young leader" category, but few people have heard of them. In spite of graduate degrees from prestigious institutions, they chose servanthood in a difficult, war-torn, poverty-stricken country where the human rewards are few. They are frequently sick, sometimes afraid for their own lives and the lives of their children, and often oppressed by the magnitude of the needs that surround them. Why do they choose this life? Stuart and Sindia are obedient; they know that love means serving.

C. S. Lewis wrote of the risks involved in loving others:

> Love anything, and your heart will certainly be wrung and possibly be broken. If you want to make sure of keeping it intact, you must give your heart to no one, not even an

> animal. Wrap it carefully round with hobbies and little luxuries; avoid all entanglements; lock it up safe in a casket or coffin of your selfishness. But in that casket—safe, dark, motionless, airless—it will change. It will not be broken; it will become unbreakable, impenetrable, irredeemable. . . .The only place outside heaven where you can be perfectly safe from all the dangers and perturbations of love is hell.[8]

Love calls us to give ourselves away and to incur the risks such giving entails. Bob could retire from ministry feeling unappreciated. Stuart and Sindia could return from their foreign home feeling fruitless. But love does not serve for results.

Christlike love takes us out of the comfort zone of living (what C. S. Lewis calls the "coffin of your selfishness"). We leave that comfort zone and enter a world of vulnerability as leaders, serving without knowing how others might respond or how the story turns out in the end.

Exemplary Love Forgives

Love serves—and becomes vulnerable—in the practice of forgiveness. When I am hurt, I am prone to hold a grudge, which is a type of emotional callous that I develop to keep myself from getting hurt again. Love forgives, cuts the callous off, and reopens the vulnerable spot.

Some are not able to rise to their potential as leaders

because they refuse to forgive someone who has hurt them in the past—a parent, parishioner, friend, or coworker. Long-term grudge-bearing makes us like boats that are moored to a dock. We may drift out a little into the open sea of leadership, but the rope of bitterness snaps us back to the dock. Sailing at our full potential never occurs until we completely release the person that has sinned against us and, in so doing, release ourselves.

Exemplary Love Empathizes

Love serves through compassion. The opposite of compassion—apathy—literally means "no feeling." It is impossible to love another and still be apathetic. True love is driven by compassion (a term that derives in the Greek from "intestines"—the connotation being that compassionate love affects us to our "gut").

Bill Hybels writes, "Empathy [or compassion] does not come naturally to us hardhearted people. We have to slow down and make a determined effort to put ourselves in other people's shoes. We need to ask ourselves how it would feel to be in their situations." Hybels continues by offering some sample compassion-building questions for the leader:

How would it feel to be handicapped, unable to stand up, walk, dress yourself, drive or even find a good seat in church because there is no room for your wheelchair?

How would it feel to be unemployed, to have a mortgage and car payments you cannot make and

to have children you cannot provide for?
How would it feel to be Black in a White community that is not particularly sensitive to minorities?
How would it feel to be divorced, to be widowed, to lose a child or parent?
How would it feel to have cancer, multiple sclerosis, Alzheimer's disease or AIDS?[9]

Compassionate love takes the time to realize that we are surrounded by the "least of these brothers of mine" (Matthew 25:40). When we empathize with their pain, we equip ourselves to serve them.

Exemplary Love Endures

Milton Friesen illustrates love in action. Every day of the year, he and his staff at Kingston House provide meals, services, and at times, lodging for the homeless of Boston. Some of these people are alcoholics; others have been released from state hospitals; all are poor. The outstanding aspect of Milton's example is his endurance. He has been serving these people for more than 20 years!

What motivates a man and his family to continue in a ministry that scares most of us away? The answer is love. "As Christ persevered in loving us," Milton will say, "so we persevere; we are only following the Lord's example."[10]

In an era of "instant" everything, we desperately need this quality of endurance. In my past youth ministry experience, endurance was the key to any effectiveness I ever achieved. In a profession where few last more than two years (at least at the same church), endurance yielded results.

And endurance communicates love. The people who come to Kingston House know that Milton loves them. Why? Because he's always there!

A friend told me the story of a youth worker who came to a church to serve and departed for another "call" four months later. In his closing address to the high school students, he said, "I want you guys to know that I really love you."

The students almost laughed, because everything he was doing contradicted his words. I can hear the students saying to themselves, "If you loved us, you wouldn't be leaving. Love doesn't quit."

THE REALMS OF LOVE

Jesus commanded love on two levels: the Lord first and "your neighbor as yourself" second. However, for better understanding, let's subdivide the latter level into "family" and "the world."

Love of God

Ultimately, our goal as leaders is to direct people to experience the love of God for themselves. Our example, however, determines whether we will be successful or not. Evelyn Underhill wrote, "You will only bring men to the love of God insofar as you yourselves have got it." She continued, "It is that love of God and that peace and presence of eternity for which souls are now so hungry; and your power of really feeding them *depends absolutely on your own secret life towards God*' (emphasis mine).[11]

A commitment to exemplary love toward God implies a recommitment to our personal devotional life. The Scriptures should be opened *daily*—for personal use, not just for preparation to teach or preach—to renew our minds and encourage our obedience. Books like *Knowledge of the Holy* (Tozer), *Knowing God* (Packer), or *Celebration of Discipline* (Foster) should be opened annually to make sure that our personal spirituality and knowledge of God are growing.

As we examine our love for God, we will pray with Archbishop George Appleton,

> O God, I know that if I do not love thee with all my heart, with all my mind, with all my soul, and with all my strength, I shall love something else with all my heart and mind and soul and strength. Grant that putting thee first in all my lovings I may be liberated from all lesser loves and loyalties, and have thee as my first love, my chiefest good and my final joy.[12]

Love of Family

The family remains one of the greatest testimonies of the gospel in practice, and every leader aspires to have family relationships that exemplify godliness. As I've said, we want our marriages and families to advertise the love of Christ.

This type of love, however, has come under great

attack with the advent of alternative lifestyles, loss of moral standing, and the ongoing incidence of divorce. Now, more than ever, young leaders must be dedicated to building families that are devoted to the principles and convictions of Scripture so that we can set positive examples for those we lead.

Exemplary love of family can compete with zeal to lead. Bob Pierce, founder of World Vision, became so preoccupied with his sense of call to the children of the world that he virtually ignored his own family. His marriage broke apart; a daughter committed suicide; he lost his health. The story, tragically recounted in Marilee Pierce Dunker's *Day of Glory*, *Seasons of Night*, vividly portrays a leader under this tension. But love for family must precede love for the "world." Dr. Tony Campolo writes, "We are successful if the most significant people in our lives deem us successful."[13] I wonder how many of us, as we grow as public figures, will stand up to the critique of spouse or children. This is the true measure of greatness.

Campolo, no stranger to the tensions and demands of a public life, writes about his own marriage in *The Power Delusion* :

> My wife and I often talk about the love we have for each other and how it came into existence. We have concluded that the reason why we love each other is because over the years each of us has given so very much to the other. Love did not happen. It was created through sacrifices and self-

> giving on the part of both of us. The more we invest in the marriage, the more precious the relationship becomes and deeper the love grows between us.[14]

Sacrifice, love, giving—these are the qualities that exemplary marriages and families are built upon.

Love for the World

Jesus Christ calls us to love our neighbors as ourselves, a demonstrated love that begins at home but carries forth into the world that we seek to serve for Christ's sake.

On one hand, we run the risk of loving the world too much. This is what happened to the Apostle Paul's coworker Demas: "Demas, because he loved this world, has deserted me" (2 Timothy 4:10). What happened? Demas evidently was enticed away from the sacrificial world of discipleship to the short-term pleasures of his day. Perhaps he settled down to a materialistically comfortable life. All we know is that he loved the world too much.

Could this happen to us? We are foolish if we think ourselves immune to temptation and the possibility of our own fall. The "cravings of sinful man, the lust of his eyes and the boasting of what he has and does" (1 John 2:16) are as real today as they were in the first century.

We could love the world too much and explicitly abandon the faith—as Demas seemed to have done. Or we can love the world in a more subtle way, while keeping an outward spiritual veneer. By flirting with evil, making choices based on Christian "fame" or prominence, or altering our values away from Christian sacrifice, we too can love our world too much.

On the other hand, we often find that we do not love the world enough. We prefer to stay in our safe Christian ghettos rather than venture forth into a world that threatens our faith.

Jerry White, general director of The Navigators, challenged a group of pastors by asking us to evaluate whether our churches were "mainstream" or "cul-de-sac" in our disciplemaking efforts.

By "mainstream" White meant a church that was aggressively involved in efforts to affect the world around it, addressing it with the gospel in understandable terms. By using "cul-de-sac" White highlighted what he thought was the principal trend in Christianity; namely, to draw people into a church as a safe place, away from the rat race and hectic pace of the mainstream, and then keep them there.

He reinforced his cul-de-sac illustration by revealing statistics that showed that most new Christians lost almost all of their non-Christian friends in their first two years as Christians.

When all of our friends are church people or fellow Christians, we live in a Christian cul-de-sac. We feel safe, but our relationships show that we love our world too little.

We can measure how much we love our world by the degree to which we *lose* something so that others might know the love of Christ. Building a relationship with a non-Christian so as to communicate the love of Christ causes us to "lose" some good Christian fellowship. Serving in our community might cause us to lose stature in our Christian "club."

Using missionaries as an example, Michael Griffiths cites five losses that occur when they go out to love the world; in some respects, these losses should characterize us all, especially leaders:

1. Loss of cultural privilege and status
2. Loss of standard of living
3. Loss of security and health
4. Loss of family and friends
5. Loss of life itself.[15]

A genuine love for the people in the world into which God calls us involves a willingness to endure loss, but also a full knowledge of Jesus' promise that "whoever loses his life for me will save it" (Luke 9:24).

CONCLUSION

Several years ago, my friend Mike and his family moved to another part of the country. He left our church at a time when our preaching pastor was considered one of the best preachers in the United States.

They moved into a small community, and the family struggled several months to find a new church. After a while, they settled on one. The attendance and programs were smaller, but the greatest struggle they had was with the preaching. In Mike's words, "We went from some of the best preaching in the United States to some of the worst."

But Mike and his family decided to join that church. He tells it this way:

> At first, the size and the preaching turned us off. We church-hopped, exploring some other churches in the area, but we kept coming back. . . . At first, we really did not understand the pull, but we felt drawn there.
>
> Then, after several Sundays, we realized that we felt drawn there because Pastor Dave loved us. He didn't coerce us to join. As a matter of fact, he would ask us how the church hunt was going—as if he were unselfishly praying for us to make the best choice for our family.
>
> Every Sunday, after the sermon, he greeted me and my family. He knew our names. He asked about the concerns in our lives. He reassured us in such a way that we *knew* he cared and was praying for us. I guess you could say that his love won us over. I suppose the sermons aren't much better, but it doesn't matter quite as much anymore. We are growing as the recipients of his love.

When we go against the selfish trends of our culture

and give of ourselves sacrificially and without reservation, we find that exemplary love draws people like a magnet.

4
Building Your Faith

The coins of the United States are engraved with this motto: In God We Trust. These powerful words reflect values of a previous generation, but do they reflect ours? Do we trust God? Are we living with the conviction that Hebrews 11:6 is true—"without faith it is impossible to please God"?

As young leaders, there are many other places where we can center our trust. But to live a life of exemplary *faith* will challenge us at the core of our spirituality.

Denny puts his trust in his youthful metabolism. He is a talented speaker, a great musician, and a good organizer. He "does it all" as a leader in his church. Anyone who watches Denny in action thinks one thing: *energy*.

Jack centers his trust on charisma and personality. He is handsome, has a voice that resounds like an operatic bass soloist, and reaches out to everyone with warmth and sensitivity. When I see Jack's personality in action, I always think the same thing: *smooth*.

Sue, on the other hand, centers her trust on her intellect. She is brilliant, having already completed (at age thirty-one) two master's degrees, a doctorate, and soon, her law degree. Her brains have afforded her countless opportunities to lead in a variety of fields. After meeting Sue, one word comes to mind: *smart.*

These three young leaders profess a faith in Jesus Christ, but the center of their faith is somewhere else. Metabolism, charisma, and knowledge have given them the ability to trust in themselves first.

While there is no sin in energy, smoothness, or smarts, putting our primary trust there is sin. The resources of enthusiasm, a great personality, or a superior intellect must be brought into submission to Christ so that we are sure we trust Him and not our own abilities.

Without faith in God, King Saul's energy was spent offering sacrifices that were not acceptable to God. Without faith in God, Nebuchadnezzar's charisma and personality were reduced to nothing as God made him a grazing madman. Without faith in God, the brilliance of first-century religious leaders blinded them from recognizing who Jesus really was.

For the exceptionally gifted person, faith is difficult. When metabolism, personality, or knowledge become the foundation of our leadership or ministry, we become prone to build our security around these external characteristics. As a result, maintaining our "image" begins to take precedence over taking risks. We grow accustomed to control, and as a result, we grow uncomfortable with faith—because faith calls us to relinquish control.

For talented people like Denny, Jack, or Sue, the

challenge to live with true "In-God-We-Trust" leadership tests their ability to put skills secondary to obedience.

For the rest of us, however, who do not feel as talented or as exceptional as these three, there remains the challenge to live by faith. We may not have the same personal resources, but we are equally prone to the desire to control or predict our lives. To act counter to this tendency requires faith.

ENEMIES OF FAITH

Timothy had to be challenged by Paul to lead others by faith. His example of faith would provide credibility to his spiritual leadership, but he was timid and reticent to take action.

We may think harshly of Timothy's hesitation as a leader—until we are willing to evaluate ourselves. Perhaps we too feel weak, incompetent to lead, or afraid of the challenges before us. We were reminded, in the introduction of this book, of the contemporary hesitancy of young men and women to assume leadership roles. Perhaps there are many "Timothys" in the twenty-five to forty age category. Our fears or feelings of inability manifest themselves in several tendencies that militate against exemplary faith.

SELF-PRESERVATION

My associate and I were evaluating my job performance, and he asked me if I was challenged with my work. I replied by explaining that, by virtue of my longevity at the same position, I had developed a high degree of competency in what I was doing.

He responded, "Yes, but just because your job is *easy* does not mean you are growing."

In his response, he had changed my word, *competency*, for his, easy. The change was subtle but poignant. He was pointing out to me why I had stopped growing in faith. I had become so competent that there was no risk left. My job was easy, and I was doing nothing to change it.

The conversation showed me how—as a relatively young man—I had already slipped into the status quo life. I might be competent, but there was no faith. I had grown accustomed to security, and now I was working to preserve it. In my desire for self-preservation, I had chosen ease over growth.

Fear of change, or the desire to "keep things the way they are," is a temptation that diffuses faith. When we work to maintain our security, we shy away from tough choices and avoid risk-taking.

The problem is not new. The rich young ruler could not throw himself totally at the mercy of Jesus because he had great riches. The more security we build for ourselves, the more we risk losing by venturing out in faith.

But leaders take risks. No one ever stubs his or her toe while standing still. Franklin D. Roosevelt once said, "It is common sense to take a method and try it. If it fails, admit it frankly. But above all, *try something*!"[1] Failing to try because of a desire to be secure results in inaction and failure to lead.

John Henry Jowett, a great English preacher, likewise

pointed out the temptation of self-preservation and its result in faithless lives:

> *It is possible to evade a multitude of sorrows through the cultivation of an insignificant life.* Indeed, if a man's ambition is to avoid the troubles of life, the recipe is simple: shed your ambitions in every direction, cut the wings of every soaring purpose, and seek a life with the fewest contacts and relations. If you want to get through the world with the smallest trouble, you must reduce yourself to the smallest compass. Tiny souls can dodge through life; bigger souls are blocked on every side. As soon as a man begins to enlarge his life, his resistances are multiplied. Let a man remove his petty selfish purposes and enthrone Christ, and his sufferings will be increased on every side (emphasis mine).[2]

The spirit of self-preservation and security effectively reduces us to settle for second best. It calls us to avoid hardship. Faith is sacrificed on the altar of safety.

"Every single day," writes Bill Hybels, "we will make choices that show whether we are courageous or cowardly. We choose between the right thing and the convenient thing, sticking to a conviction or caving in for the sake of comfort, greed, or approval. *We choose either to take a carefully thought out risk* [faith] *or to crawl into a shrinking shell of safety, security and inactivity*" (emphasis mine).[3]

The desire to stay safe, at ease, or secure will lure us away from a life of faith.

HOPELESSNESS

Tony Campolo spends an enormous amount of time exhorting young people to realize that they can make a difference. Why? Because average young people today do not believe that they can. The spirit of Ecclesiastes—that all is emptiness and in vain—has made its home in the hearts of many young people. Like ten of the twelve spies sent into the Promised Land, they see the obstacles of our age as insurmountable. Like Saul and his men before Goliath, they feel too insignificant and impotent to act.

We fall prey to hopelessness when we focus on the immensity of world need. Within seven days of having first written these pages, an earthquake in Armenia has killed 70,000 and left 500,000 homeless, and I learned of civil war in Sri Lanka, flooding in Bangladesh, and starvation in Sudan. At home, two people we knew have died of cancer, and many of the people of the nearby city of Boston will have no Christmas to celebrate because they are homeless. If my trust were centered in my own ability to respond to these needs, I would become hopeless, pessimistic, or cynical.

Hopelessness likewise overtakes us when we trust in Christian leaders rather than in Christ. I was in Kathmandu, the capital of the Hindu Kingdom of Nepal, just as the tragic revelations of financial mismanagement at the PTL Ministry were becoming public (summer 1987). In a country where Christianity is facing overwhelming challenges, the four-page English newspaper contained a front-page article about the auctioning of the air-conditioned doghouse that the PTL founders had had specially built for their poodle. If my faith were in Christian leaders, I would have given up that day.

Hopelessness might manifest itself in pessimism or cynicism or inactivity, but all are enemies of the life of faith. Through faith, we believe that God will work in our world, and amazingly, He wants to use us.

Unhealthy Imitation

Much of our growth in Christ comes as a result of imitation. The principle of imitation "Follow Me"—is basic to discipleship. Choosing a good mentor will emerge as a theme later in the book, but there are some unhealthy aspects of the mentoring/discipleship model that can harm our growth in faith.

Faith suffers when we imitate other Christians too much. Some Christians—especially younger ones—can choose older Christian mentors whom they adore like Indian gurus. The discipler's word becomes truth, and the disciple follows without question. This unhealthy dependence distracts the younger believer from imitating the Bereans, who "examined the Scriptures every day to see if what Paul said was true" (Acts 17:11). If disciples are not evaluating the life and teachings of their discipler according to the Scriptures, the followers can be led astray.

Faith likewise suffers when Christians imitate each other's methods without prayer. Peter Lord explained this unhealthy imitation at a conference for church leaders. I have paraphrased his remarks:

> Church A is praying for revival. In the midst of that fervent prayer, God directs Church A to develop Methodology A to reach their community.
>
> If Church A is obedient, they develop and implement Methodology A, and—because it is God's plan—Methodology A gets results. People are converted and Church A is enlarged.
>
> Church A then becomes a model for other churches. They send their pastor or lay leaders to revival seminars to explain their own growth through Methodology A. Other churches read about Methodology A in Christian publications, and they buy Methodology A manuals to implement it in their own churches.
>
> Churches B, C, and D implement Methodology A, and all three get some results, but *without prayer, without waiting on God, and without genuine revival.* They get some results because Methodology A is from God, but they might miss God's best because they imitated Church A rather than waiting on God in

prayer, by faith asking Him for His plan for their churches.

Through this example, Peter Lord points out that by imitating the success of others, we may miss God's best for our own individual situation. In his example, churches B, C, and D *might* have been directed by the Holy Spirit to use Methodology A, but their imitation without prayer and faith was motivated by a desire to get results by copying the techniques of others.[4]

Temporal Thinking

Many people of our materialistic Western culture are living as if this life is all there is. Even Christians focus their attention on this life rather than on what will last for eternity. We have life so comfortable here, we think (although we might not admit it to our church friends), "I wonder if Heaven will be this good" (or, as one beer commercial puts it, "It doesn't get any better than this!").

Part of my work is to educate and encourage people to leave their comforts to go out in missionary service. Of all the excuses that are offered, the most common reflect on "all that I'd have to leave," or how "it's so dangerous there." Both excuses reflect thinking that is concentrated on things present rather than on things to come, things temporal rather than things eternal.

Again, this struggle to think with an eternal perspective is not new. Paul exhorted the Colossians to "set your minds on things above, not on earthly things" (Colossians 3:2). John reminded his disciples "the world and its desires pass away, but the man who does the will of God lives forever"(1 John 2:17).

Thomas á Kempis addressed temporary thinking as an enemy of faith in the opening chapter of his book, *The Imitation of Christ*:

> It is vanity, therefore, to seek riches, and to trust in that which is perishable.
>
> It is vanity, too, to seek for honors, and to strive for high positions.
>
> It is vanity to follow the desires of the flesh, and to crave for that which would inevitably bring with it a sore punishment.
>
> It is vanity to wish for length of life, and to care little that the life should be well spent.
>
> It is vanity to think only of the present life, and not to provide for the future.
>
> It is vanity to love that which swiftly passes away, and not to hasten onwards to that place where joy abides forever.[5]

NEEDED: LEADERS WITH VISION

Fulfilling his pastoral duties required Timothy to lead by exemplary faith. What did this faith look like for Timothy? What will it look like for us?

Leaders with Vision Are People of the Word

The Bible offers us many examples of faith—men

and women who had their vision set on God and His Kingdom, and whose vision was reflected in their lives, decisions, and priorities.

Joseph exemplified unconditional faith in God's sovereignty, believing that "God meant it for good" even when his brothers' actions led him to prison and alienation in a foreign land. David lived as a man after God's own heart. Daniel exemplified courage in the face of opposition. Mary, the mother of Jesus, willingly lost her reputation (and her dreams of marriage, at least temporarily) to obey God. Jesus Christ taught us to be gentle with the hurting person and the outcast. Paul illustrated a life fully given over to Christ. John gave us the vision of Heaven.

To be people of vision, we must know the people of the Bible: "For everything that was written in the past was written to teach us, so that through endurance and the encouragement of the Scriptures we might have hope" (Romans 15:4).

We, as leaders who desire to live by faith, must be aware of the great "cloud of witnesses" (Hebrews 12:1) who have gone before us, who "by faith" (Hebrews 11) were the people of vision for their time.

"Faith," wrote A.W. Tozer, "is simply the bringing of our minds into accord with the truth. It is adjusting our expectations to the promises of God in complete assurance that the God of the whole earth cannot lie."[6] To bring our minds in accordance with the truth, we must know God's Word.

Charles Blair tells of his own downfall as pastor of Calvary Temple in *The Man Who Could Do No*

Wrong. The momentum of growth and the glorious new accomplishments of their church caused him and others to move forward—even past God. He relates how the successes of the past led them forward with such fury that mistakes were made leading to devastating financial mismanagement.

In retrospect, Blair advises leaders to check their dreams and visions by asking, "Is the dream HIS vision? Is the method HIS way? Is the timing HIS moment?"[7] The only way to submit ourselves to these evaluations is through thorough submission to God's Word.

Christians from the United States who serve as missionaries in the developing countries often return home with tales of great miracles and movements of the Spirit of God. One leader told me the story of the outpouring of the gospel in India. He said, "You know, these people aren't like you and me; *they really believe the Bible*! When God says, 'Do it,' they obey. They cast out demons, see people healed, and believe God for miracles. They don't have all of our twentieth century explanations and rationalizations for the Bible. They believe that God will act as He did at Pentecost, and He does!"

Every leader must start in the development of his or her faith with the key question: *Do I really believe the Bible?*

Leaders with Vision Take Risks

In the late 1980s, I came to know Caesar and Ajith. I met them first at a conference, and then both came to study in the United States, where our acquaintance was renewed. Both were preparing to return to their homes, although they could stay in the comforts of the United States and assume leadership positions in reputable Christian organizations.

Their decision to return home involved great courage. Both are married and have young children. Both returned to places where their lives and their children's are endangered. Caesar walked back into the increasing restlessness of a South African township, where he was opposed by the white minority government because he favored the abolition of apartheid and by fellow black leaders because he did not endorse violence.

Ajith returns to Columbo, Sri Lanka, an island torn by civil war, where he could be killed by radical communist groups who are violently opposed to Christianity. They believe Christianity is an expression of Western imperialism.

Why do they return? Ultimately, they are driven by their faith in Jesus Christ who has called them to these lands. They sacrifice the comforts of a life in the United States and subject themselves and their families to great danger because they walk by faith.

While most of us will not face the risk-taking decisions that Caesar and Ajith confront, we all must take risks if we are to lead. Faith is trusting God when the results are not predictable or assured. If there is no risk, then leadership will be, at best, maintenance, and there will be no need for faith. Without risk, we will live in what Teddy Roosevelt called "the gray twilight that knows neither victory nor defeat."

Faith begins when we yield ourselves to God. In

The Power Delusion, Dr. Tony Campolo distinguishes faith from magic. Magic, he says, is when we try to get spiritual control so that God acts on our behalf; it is, in effect, trying to dictate the actions of spiritual forces. Faith, in contrast, is yielding us to a higher power's control. Faith involves the *relinquishing* of control; magic seeks to acquire control.[8]

In the first century AD, John Chrysostom yielded his life to Christ, and in the process of that submission, he felt called by God to speak out against rich people who acted callously toward the poor. This was a substantial risk, since the empress was known for her opulence and yet her support of the clergy. His speaking out in obedience to God resulted in his exile by the empress and deposition as a church leader.

Yet his faith prevailed. Terry Muck points out in *When to Take a Risk* that the empress "is now a footnote in history," but Chrysostom's writings "have influenced countless theologians in the fifteen centuries since his death."[9]

Why do we fail to take risks of faith? Fear of failure can paralyze us to adhering to the status quo. Perhaps we wonder if God will deliver us. Perhaps there is a fear of death or physical pain or, more realistically, of public ridicule or social embarrassment.

As young leaders, we need to develop the quality of faith so that we grow accustomed to the risks involved in following Jesus Christ. It might start with little risks:

- to reach out to a hurting person without knowing how much energy it will take;

- to attempt to lead even though others seem comfortable to remain at a standstill;
- to share ourselves with others at the risk of being hurt;
- to teach, even though we might be ignored;
- to share the gospel, even when the results are quite unpredictable.

Growing accustomed to small risks gradually helps us to develop our faith "muscles." The stronger we get, the larger the risks we are empowered to take. As we grow in faith, we will stretch our ability to step into situations where only God can deliver us.

David Howard shares a story in *What Makes a Missionary*? that illustrates the aversion to faith and risk-taking sometimes present in young people. A young man met David and told him, "Well, I'm disqualified now for missions."

"Why?" David Howard asked.

"Well, I'm thirty-two," the young man replied.

His answer implied a settling in for the status quo, a commitment to safety and the comforts of adult life. "Since I made it past thirty without being called to a life of faith," the young man seemed to be saying, "I can now settle down to security and peace."[10]

That young man may reflect a spirit of our times, but he is far from the risk-taking spirit needed for exemplary faith in the Church.

People of Faith Dream Dreams

The phrase "I have a dream" echoed through one of

Martin Luther King's most memorable sermons. He had a dream, and he lived—and died—to further the fulfillment of the dream, making him one of the most influential leaders of the twentieth century.

He had a dream, and many other men and women of faith in the 1950s had dreams as well. Bob Pierce dreamed of meeting the needs of thousands of orphans worldwide, and he lived to see that dream fulfilled through World Vision International. Billy Graham had dreams of touching lives with the gospel, and he became the greatest evangelist of Christian history. Bill Bright had dreams of reaching college students for Christ, and Campus Crusade for Christ was born. The 1950s was an exciting decade of young leaders who dreamed dreams.

But the next generation became managers of the dreams of others. Rather than dreaming new dreams, they served as the administrators of the dreams of the generation before them. As a result, many great movements were developed—but there were not as many new dreams. In some situations, the spirit of "maintenance" overtook visions of faith.

The need now is for a new generation of those who will dream dreams. The challenge for young leaders is to develop a walk with Christ that gives vision to what God wants to do through them. We need people who will dream dreams about how the Church can minister to those with AIDS. We need dreamers of new ways to reach people in parts of the world that are inaccessible to the gospel. We need innovators, spiritual "inventors" that will—by faith—dream dreams of God's work being accomplished in ways that are uniquely relevant to our times.

The dreams of our generation might not take the shape of dreams of the past, and we must make sure to get God's new dreams for us—not simply mimicking those of past generations. Only a few will be called to the worldwide visibility of people like Billy Graham, Bob Pierce, or Bill Bright, but all of us are called to dream dreams about what God can do through our lives.

When I was a teenager, older people invested in me and gave me a desire to reach out to those in need. Their investment in me caused me to dream that I might do the same for others when I became a youth worker. Twelve years ago, I began to pray that God would use me to influence others to go out in service all over the world. My dream was to be able to take a year later in life to travel around the world, visiting alumni of our ministry here.

I do not know whether I will ever get to take that trip, but I do know that God is working to fulfill that dream. Cindy is in Honduras. Paul and Lorie, and Wendy, are in Japan—and Jeff leaves soon. Dan and Sarah are preparing for Venezuela, and Jim and Sherry are planning for North Africa. Others are getting ready for other locations in Africa, Europe, Asia, Latin America, and parts of the United States.

The fulfilled dream is God's work through me and dozens of others who caught the vision to be missions-mobilizers. We had the dream, acted on faith, and God gave the results.

Michael Griffiths writes of the courageous dreams of the people of Acts as they reached out to others. He concludes with this challenge:

> We are not to stay in our social and religious ghettos, but to venture out boldly in the power of the Spirit to stay with tanners, hitch-hike with Ethiopians, dance for joy with beggars, feast with tax-collectors, embrace Samaritans as brothers and to be liberated from the fetters of our social and ethnic reserve by the missionary Christ . . . *The Outgoing God, then, calls us to wildness and risk and humility and love* (emphasis mine).[11]

What is your dream of faith?

FAITH BUILDING

How can we grow in our faith? How do we develop a deeper ability to trust God, even when the outcome of leadership decisions is not clear?

Faith is the gift of God (Ephesians 2:8-9). Now that we have received that gift, it is our responsibility to exercise it, develop it, and provide opportunities for faith to grow.

Faith grows when we make some fundamental life commitments.

COMMITMENT 1: TO GROW IN THE BASICS

As a basketball fan, I have enjoyed watching a variety of professional players, but Julius Erving ("Dr. J") was one of my favorites. His ability to maneuver his body through a crowd while holding the basketball with one hand and then complete the move by "stuffing" the ball through the hoop would bring any crowd to its feet. He was certainly one of the most colorful players in NBA history.

When Julius Erving was at his prime, his moves and gymnastic feats were copied by many young players. On playgrounds and in gymnasiums everywhere, high school and college players would try to imitate his most dazzling moves. But most forgot one truth about Julius Erving: It was not the dazzling moves that made him great.

The dazzling moves were a cumulative result of his commitment to basketball basics—lay-ups, jumping, dribbling, using other players as "picks," shooting foul shots, making good passes, playing defense. He became an all-star because he matched his abilities with a mastering of the basics. Young players who wanted to do the colorful moves without the basics could not make the team. Coaches wanted students who were committed to the basics, not to showmanship.

The same is true in our spiritual growth. We may see those we consider spiritual "all-stars"—men and women past and present—whose greatest spiritual feats we want to imitate. So, like the young players imitating Dr. J's most dazzling moves, we start by trying to do the impressive or the notable works of faith.

But, like those young basketball players, we will find ourselves unable to do the great feats if we are weak in the spiritual basics. If our "fundamentals" of spiritual discipline are not in order, we will not have the abilities to perform under pressure or in the face of extraordinary challenges.

When we look at men and women of faith, we find that most were committed to the spiritual basics long before God made them great. They were learning worship while they were shepherds (like Moses or David); they were developing a heart for evangelism and missions while repairing boots at a cobbler's shop (like William Carey); they were learning prayer in the obscurity of a prison camp (like Corrie ten Boom).

Hudson Taylor said, "God chose to use me because I was small enough."[12] In anonymity, Taylor was faithful to the basic disciplines of obedience, and then God made him great.

Basic discipline number one must be worship. As we humble ourselves before God, He promises to give us grace (James 4:6). Worship leads both to a sense of helplessness and a renewed sense of dependence on God. Until we sense our absolute dependence on God, there will be no revival in our lives. Only when we come openhanded before God, praying the prayer of the hymn-writer—"Nothing in my hand I bring; simply to Thy cross I cling"—will God fully reveal His greatest purposes to us.

E. Stanley Jones of India wrote, "Prayer is surrender—surrender to the will of God and cooperation with that will. If I throw out a boat hook from the boat and catch hold of the shore and pull, do I pull the shore to me, or do I pull myself to the shore? Prayer is not pulling God to my will, but the aligning of my will to the will of God."[13]

Worship likewise reduces us so that we do not think too highly of ourselves or our abilities. Realizing the majesty of God, we will refrain from any consideration of ourselves as "great." Gordon MacDonald writes that "an unguarded strength and an unprepared heart are double weaknesses."[14] Worship addresses both weaknesses, helping us to see our strengths realistically and preparing our hearts before God.

Basic discipline number two is study. Without a regular diet of the Bible and consistent exposure to Christian literature, we will stunt our spiritual growth. Have we read any new books lately? How is the daily discipline of Scripture study or memorization coming along? Is it time to return to a spiritual classic like Augustine's *Confessions* or William Law's *Serious Call to a Devout and Holy Life*?

In my own life, I have become increasingly aware of my ability to "bluff" others spiritually. After we have been Christians for five or six years or more, we learn how to say the "right" spiritual things and use the "right" words in our prayers. I have come to the realization that I could bluff my way through the remaining years of my life without any new growth or input. Simply by repeating old themes or by changing my audience (like those that change churches every two or three years), I could maintain a position of spiritual leadership without any new study or personal growth. (It is a frightening thought, but I believe it is possible.) A commitment to study keeps me from stagnating.

Basic discipline number three is relationships. When I went searching for definitions of leadership, I found only one uniformly accepted understanding: A leader is one who has followers. Relationships are basic to the notion of leadership.

Yet relationships can suffer most when we lead. We can ignore our relationships at home so that spouse and family yearn for our attention. We can grow harsh and impatient with co-workers as we dedicate ourselves to some significant task. We can even come to the point where we ignore our relationship with God as we seek to serve Him.

This brings us back to worship. Effective spiritual leadership requires us to operate with a strong sense of who we are before God so that we can relate to others in that light. If we forget the grace of God toward us, we are more likely to communicate acceptance toward others based on their performance. If we are motivated by guilt, we may try to motivate others similarly. If we forget the forgiveness of God, we may forget to forgive those who trespass against us.

Kent Hughes offers some healthy evaluative questions in *Liberating Ministry from the Success Syndrome* that can help us make sure we are concentrating on the basics with God:

1. Am I believing that God can take care of me?
2. Am I believing that He loves me?

3. Am I believing that He rewards, that He is morally active on the part of those who seek Him?[15]

Our answers to these questions put us face to face with our personal faith in God—and this is most basic of all.

Commitment 2: To Stay Fresh

A man my age came in to counsel with me. He felt that his life was directionless, and in his wanderings he was driving his wife crazy. She convinced him to come see me. He arrived, settled down with a cup of coffee, and we began talking.

He did most of the talking. All I said was, "Tell me about yourself," and he obliged me happily. He showed me newspaper clippings of his past athletic feats and a college championship ring. He told me of academic performance and the Ivy League school from which he graduated Phi Beta Kappa.

After about thirty-five minutes, he took a breath—enough time for me to say something. I asked, "Tell me about the present—your family, your career, anything."

"There's not much to tell," he responded with a distant look, as if he were still thinking about that college championship. "It's pretty much been boring since college." Then he snapped out of his daze, realized what he had said, and proceeded to add some nice comments about his wife, their children, and the Christian life.

But I realized that he had told me more about himself

in the unguarded remark than in his previous statements. He was bored. Adulthood was not nearly as stimulating as college, and at age thirty-five, he had regressed to living in past memories. He had past laurels of success, and he was content to live on those.

All of us face the realistic challenges of adult life sometime in our late twenties or early thirties. We find that success in adulthood is not really as exciting as it was in college. We find that the house we dreamed of owning has a leaky basement—on the same day that our beautiful new car won't start. A friend summed it up: "In college, you have long-term plans, creative goals, and objectives; in early adulthood, you learn that a realistic long-term goal might be 'to make it till the weekend.'"

Adult life is a challenge for which many young people feel ill-prepared, but it is here that our commitment to spiritual discipline must take effect. In the midst of our early adult disillusionment, we must make the commitment to keep on growing—to stay fresh. My contemporary had not made that choice, and now, at thirty-five, he was bored, unfulfilled, and restless.

We can make the choice if we commit ourselves (and recommit daily) to grow as Christian men and women. Staying fresh includes study about our culture and the trends in our world. Without such study, we will not be able to address the gospel to the modern mind.

Staying fresh likewise includes the cultivation of creativity. After I read the biography of Dawson Trotman, founder of The Navigators, I remembered one of his shortest prayers. When he sensed that his vision was waning or he was getting spiritually stale, he would pray, "God, give me an idea!"[16] All of us would be wise to pray that prayer to keep from the temptation of living on past accomplishments or memories.

Staying fresh must include the cultivation of our spirit as well. As men and women seeking to point others to God, we cannot afford to lag in our own zeal for Him. "Leadership is exciting and exacting," Chua Wee Hian writes, "and spiritual leaders have to give themselves unstintingly to meet the needs of their people. *Unless our inner lives are renewed and replenished, there will be little depth to our ministry*" (emphasis mine).[17]

COMMITMENT 3: TO STEP OUT

A cute poster shows a small turtle shyly moving ahead; the caption reads: "Behold the turtle who moves forward only by sticking his neck out." Moving ahead requires us to stick our necks out, to take risks, to rely on God in ways never before imagined.

Some will be called to step out in faith in the face of great personal hurt. Our families may have prepared us for leadership, or—as is true of many young adults in our world today—we may have come out of families that are called "dysfunctional." Perhaps a father was abusive or a mother was alcoholic. Perhaps our parents related to us in ways that caused deep emotional pain. To think of being a leader, of "rising to the challenge," is very difficult for those who have lived their childhood years in pain.

Yet it is possible. By faith, we can trust God to begin the healing process. He can provide us with assurance of love even if we never knew it in our homes. He can lead us to proper confidence even if insecure parents berated us.

Paul Tournier, in the book *Creative Suffering*, cites a study by Dr. Pierre Rentchnick in 1975 in which he revealed that almost 300 of the greatest names in history had been orphans. Many leaders—including Alexander the Great, Julius Caesar, Golda Meir, Hitler, Castro, Lenin, Eva Peron, and Stalin—had "suffered in childhood from emotional deprivation."[18]

This list started me thinking of biblical characters who suffered similarly: Joseph was abandoned by his brothers at a young age and sold into slavery; Moses was a childhood refugee in the Egyptian palace; Daniel and his comrades became political prisoners in their early teens. Many of the greatest biblical leaders suffered some emotional deprivation as they grew up.

The choice that those in pain face as they contemplate the challenge is whether to use the pain to bring healing to others (as Joseph or Daniel did) or to dominate or hurt others (as some of those mentioned in the Rentchnick study did).

Others will be called to step out in faith in the face of danger. As my friends Caesar and Ajith illustrate, many will be called to walk into dangerous conditions if the work of the gospel is to be accomplished.

Several friends have obeyed God by going out as foreign missionaries into tropical jungles. They have survived malaria, parasites, and guerrilla warfare, but they are very aware of the dangers. Others serve in the urban United States, facing the dangers of faith there as they actively work with police to stop drug dealers. They live under constant threat of death, but they step out in faith.

The world of the early twenty-first century will be increasingly hostile to the gospel, and as a result, many will face physical danger in order to remain faithful to the Lord. Are we ready?

Listen again to Michael Griffiths as he addresses the reality of faith-risks in *What on Earth Are You Doing*?

> Are you willing to go anywhere for Jesus Christ? If you have as good an imagination as I have, you can lose a lot of sleep over the question. Does the Lord want me to go and preach to the Eskimos and perhaps freeze to death in the Arctic? I heard of a missionary who dived into the Amazon river for a swim and all that came to the surface was his bathing trunks! If I went to Latin American I might be eaten alive by piranha, man-eating fish. Or does the Lord perhaps want me to go to India, where I might catch cholera and be dehydrated to death?

Griffiths concludes with some realistic humor:

> If you are imagining all the frightening

> situations you might meet or all the horrible deaths you might die, I have a word of encouragement for you. You cannot possibly die in all these different ways—only in one of them! Let's get our foolish fear in proportion . . . . Death is a possibility today wherever we live.[19]

A.W. Tozer summarized the Christian's faith by defining the Christian life with the term "the wind in our face." "The wind is in Christ's face, and because we go with him we too shall have the wind in our face. We should not expect less."[20]

If we step out in the discipline of faith, we will be leaning into a stiff opposing wind, but Jesus will be there by our side!

CONCLUSION

When we seek to live by exemplary faith, we put ourselves at the mercy of God. We are commanded to walk by faith, not by sight—but it's uncomfortable to be unsure about where our next step will lead. Nevertheless, we step out in faith, believing that God is the rewarder of those who diligently seek Him (Hebrews 11:6).

Charles Swindoll, in *A Quest for Character*, issues a challenge that aptly concludes this chapter:

Vision. It is essential for survival. It is spawned by faith, sustained by hope, sparked by imagination and strengthened by enthusiasm. It is greater than sight, deeper than a dream, broader than an idea. Vision encompasses vast vistas outside the realm of the predictable, the safe, the expected. No wonder we perish without it! Ask God to stretch your vision today—to encourage you with visionary plans as you walk in his presence.[21]

5
A Commitment to Purity

Has purity ceased to exist? This is what we are tempted to believe as we consider leadership—both in the world and, sadly, in the Church. A pastor of a 10,000-member church recently resigned, citing an adulterous relationship with a church member as the reason. A key Christian leader underwent the scrutiny of the Christian public as discussion continued about his home—Did it cost $1 million or $2 million?

Denominations wrestle with whether or not they should ordain homosexuals. Television evangelists go to court to protect their "kingdoms." In leadership outside the Church, immorality, scandals, defrauding, and double-dealing seem to characterize the news. As a people, we seem to be what the Bible would call "defiled." Charles Colson said, "If God does not punish the United States, he owes Sodom and Gomorrah an apology."[1]

A poll by *U.S. News and World Report* and CNN reported that more than half of over 1,000 people surveyed thought people are less honest today than they were ten years before. Seven out of ten say that they are dissatisfied with current standards of honesty—the largest proportion since the Watergate scandal of 1973.[2] Only 38 percent believed that the president "tells it like it is."[3]

Purity is hard to find, whether in financial management or sexual control. We sail as a culture without a moral compass, and as a result, we find ourselves adrift in a sea of relativism.

But in the face of such standards (or lack thereof), books like Campolo's *The Power Delusion* and Foster's *Money, Sex and Power* call us to reevaluate. As Paul challenged Timothy, these leaders (and others) call us to purity—of life, of sexuality, of Christian consistency.

A CALL TO PURITY

There is no greater test of our exemplary leadership than this matter of purity. To be pure is to be free from corruption, free from error or flaw. We might respond to the challenge of purity with the Pauline phrase, "Who is adequate for these things?" (2 Corinthians 2:16, NASB).

Tokunboh Adeyemo, general secretary of the Association of Evangelicals of Africa and Madagascar, wrote of his predecessor, Byang Kato, "His life as a prophet was marked by courage, boldness, moral purity and discipline. His message was forthright, powerful, uncompromising but always compassionate."[4] Adeyemo described a young leader who exemplified a life of purity. To live such a life is possible—by the power of the Holy Spirit.

THE CALL TO SEXUAL PURITY

Confronting the "demon of lust" may make the difference between effectiveness as a leader and a hasty retreat from leadership. We do not have to search far for stories of great (or potentially great) leaders who disappeared from leadership because they lost the battle to the demon of lust. When we hear of these leaders, we are wise to step back and ask: How can I keep from losing that same battle?

I entered a discussion with a ministerial friend after we both had heard the story of a pastor who had committed adultery. He responded to the story confidently. "I don't understand this rash of immorality in the ministry," he said. "I committed my sexuality to the Lord, and I have not struggled with lustful temptation since."

The man's confidence scared me. Perhaps he was telling the truth, but my personal experience and my discussions with many others led me to believe he was being naive (or worse, deceiving himself). I remembered an eighty-year-old speaker who had come to our church several years earlier. It was summer, and people were wearing comfortable clothes—including some short shorts. He started his seminar with this prayer: "Oh, God, deliver me from lustful thinking!"

The confident response of my friend and the prayer of this eighty-year-old man of God helped me to see the tension every leader faces. The younger man desperately wanted to appear spiritual in addressing his sexual drives; the older, wiser man was simply honest before God. That older man helped me distinguish the difference between "winning the battle" and "having won the battle." Our goal—sexual purity—calls us to ask God to help us to be winning in the battle of lust. We shall not win the final battle until we see Jesus face to face.

So how can we be winning the battle in sexual purity, even though victory might not be complete in this life? Several basic commitments before God can help keep us on the victorious side.

Commitment 1: Personal Purity

Impure images, fantasies, and lustful thoughts are the enemies of our soul according to Peter (1 Peter 2:11). We must cry out to God for the power to make a covenant with our eyes not to look lustfully at another, following the example of righteous Job (Job 31:1). "By God's power," writes Kent Hughes, "we must covenant not to view anything that would pull us down from holiness to sensuality, whether in printed material, in the media, or in life."[5]

Our minds function like cameras; once we record an image, it's difficult to erase it. Scotty, a younger Christian, was walking with older Christian men when they approached the marquee of a pornographic theater. Scotty read the signs as he had done before, but when he turned around, his friends were across the street. The older men had crossed the street to avoid recording the mental images of those signs. They explained that they ran from all such imagery whenever possible so that it would not return to their minds later.

The thought of "running" from sexual lusts is a good one. This is exactly what Joseph did when he was seduced by Potiphar's wife (Genesis 39:6-12). The Bible does not say Joseph was not tempted, it simply tells us that he ran. David should have done the same when he saw Bathsheba, but his failure to run from temptation caused him to run to adultery.

In his second letter to Timothy, Paul reminded him that he needed to "flee the evil desires of youth" (2 Timothy 2:22), or it can be translated to "flee youthful lusts." However we translate it, the concept of "fleeing"—or running—is the same.

A collegian came to me for counsel because he was unable to overcome his sexual fantasies. I asked him to tell me more, but my counsel was fruitless; that is, until I visited his dormitory room. Beside his bed he had a stack of pornographic literature. "Are these yours?" I asked. "Yes," he said. "I read them to try to relieve my lustful desires."

"Get rid of them!" I said, trying not to raise my voice. "It is no wonder you are having lustful thoughts if this is what you are feeding your mind. You have to learn to run from images like these, not to them."

We have been bought with a price, and this is our motivation for sexual purity (1 Corinthians 6:20). We no longer belong to ourselves; we belong to Jesus, who purchased us. Therefore, we aim at glorifying God with our bodies.

A commitment to personal purity—glorifying God with our bodies—means, therefore,

- a commitment to run from destructive pictures, literature, innuendoes, humor;
- a commitment to be honest with ourselves and God, not minimizing our struggles with feigned spirituality;
- a commitment to refrain from rationalizations (like, "I'm reading pornography to help satiate my sexual needs").

Eugene Habecker offers these helpful tips for the business traveler in his book *The Other Side of Leadership*:

> First, since the eyes and the mind are critically involved with lust, leaders ought to avoid "stopping to gaze" at hotel and airport-newsstands. Buy the newspaper and run. Second, when in a hotel room, consider not turning on the TV and rely instead on the radio. Too many times I have found myself tempted to watch an HBO movie ("Of course I can handle it"), so I have learned that the best defense is simply not to watch the TV. Third, always keep your spouse informed of time spent out of the office with a member of the opposite sex, whether lunch, business trip, or otherwise.[6]

COMMITMENT 2: RELATIONAL PURITY

Rick, a fellow youth worker, came on our high

school retreat; he wanted to see how we ran our program. He brought a student leader from his youth group, a young woman in the eleventh-grade.

On the bus ride home, Pam, one of my own students, approached me looking concerned. She had noticed something about Rick and his youth group member that really bothered her. "Did you notice how many times he hugged her?" she asked. I said, "Yes" (but I had hoped that my student had not noticed).

This bothered Pam and other youth group members because they knew Rick's wife and his two children. "I guess they just seemed too physical for a youth leader and youth group member," Pam continued. "Would you speak to him?"

Rick hindered his example as a leader because of indiscretion with this young woman from his youth group. When I confronted him, he explained how she was a needy student who (in his opinion) looked at him as a father figure. I responded, "But you're only ten years older than she is, and she is a *woman*, not a little girl.

Rick got defensive and the conversation concluded, but it reminded me of Paul's exhortation to Timothy that he treat "older women as mothers, and younger women as sisters, *with absolute purity*" (1 Timothy 5:2, emphasis mine).

Relational purity with members of the opposite sex who are not our spouses can be a tension in a day when so many gender barriers have been (positively) broken down. Nevertheless, we are still called to purity, and this means

- making sure to avoid indiscreet touches or excessive physical contact;
- avoiding suggestive remarks or double-meaning humor;
- meeting one-on-one in public rather than private locations (and telling our spouse about the meeting, as Habecker suggests);
- avoiding fostering unhealthy dependence in those we counsel.

Commitment 3: Marital Purity

Several years ago, a person who had been significant in my life as a mentor and leader resigned from Christian leadership because of an adulterous relationship. I was deeply grieved. Shortly after the resignation, I met with him for reconciliation and counsel. In the course of a very healing conversation, I asked him for his advice on how to avoid a similar fall. He offered some insights and summarized his advice with these words: *Don't do it!*

Good advice from one who found out the hard way. Don't do it! Marital purity is not a decision we make in the face of weakness or passion. We make it at the outset of our marriage, and we renew it every day: Don't do it! Don't be unfaithful! Don't let the sexual realm of our marriage falter! Don't take on so many Christian responsibilities that intimacy is lost!

Don't engage in crude humor or affectionate touches with someone else's spouse. Don't wander down the road named "fantasy." Don't invite temptation. If we will lead by example in the realm of sexual purity, we must strive to maintain proper intimacy with our spouse. Only then will we have the reserve to respond "Don't do it!" in a critical moment of temptation.

A Special Word to Singles

Those who will face some of the greatest struggles with sexual purity are the men and women that God calls to be single—either for a lifetime or for a period of time in adult life. The never-married or formerly-married live in a world where sexual immorality is more acceptable, thus intensifying their challenge.

The only word of encouragement that I can give to those of you who are single is this: The rules don't change with the times! Even if you think that everybody else is sexually active, God's call is to restraint. There are no exceptions; there are no special dispensations to accommodate sexual drives. Sexual relations outside of the marriage relationship are sin.

Bill was well known in some Christian circles because of his column in a nationwide Christian magazine. I knew him only from a distance, but he seemed to be a fine, single lay-leader in his church. That's what I thought—until I talked with some people from near Bill's home. They told me that Bill was known for his live-in girlfriends (yes, plural). He had changed to a liberal denomination that would accommodate his behavior, but his sexual lifestyle was in sharp contrast to biblical standards.

How could this be? I suppose that there could be a number of explanations of how Bill had drifted away from standards of biblical purity, but the largest reason was that he had convinced himself that the rules changed with the times. "This is the modern era," he said, "and you cannot expect me to live by dated puritanical ideals."

What I expected was not the issue. The issue is what God expects, and He has called us to purity.

THE CALL TO FINANCIAL PURITY

Richard Foster calls our struggle with money the "demon of greed."[7] In leadership, we are faced with great financial temptations—especially in affluent Western culture. Yet, in direct confrontation with the demon of greed, Paul tells Timothy that a Christian leader must not be a "lover of money" (1 Timothy 3:3). He adds in that same letter,

> People who want to get rich fall into temptation and a trap and into many foolish and harmful desires that plunge men into ruin and destruction. For the love of money is a root of all kinds of evil. Some people, eager for money, have wandered from the faith and pierced themselves with many griefs. (1 Timothy 6:9-10)

Purity in our leadership will reflect on our attitude toward money and how we administer the material resources we have. Unfortunately, the testimony of our age is often the opposite of purity. Embezzlement, financial mismanagement, and a lust for personal wealth are reported regularly—even in the Christian news.

"Some of the best fiction of our day can be found on the expense reports of Christian Organizations."[8] If this is true, it depicts how far we have wandered from financial integrity.

Again the question arises, how can we prevent the same from happening to us? Some leaders do well in business and find themselves with more money than they ever thought possible. Others in Christian ministries may be amazed by the power of a sermon or the appeal of a fund-raising letter to solicit monies. How can we keep from being enticed by that demon of greed?

Consider two more commitments.

Commitment 1: Ethics

There is a fictional story, which is commonly told, of three men who faced ethical financial choices after a friend gave a large amount of cash to each and later died. The dying man had asked them to place the money in his casket before he was buried. After the funeral, the three men gathered together. After some conversation about the dead man, the first trustee blurted out that he had put some— but not all—of the money in the casket. The second trustee felt likewise convicted and told a similar story. The third man spoke in pious condemnation. "Friends," he said. "I am ashamed of you. I want you to know that I put my personal check for the entire amount in the casket this morning." Each one had failed ethically, with the pious trustee being the worst of all.

The Evangelical Commission on Financial

Accountability (ECFA) has been formed to help Christian organizations operate by acceptable ethical standards with respect to financial management. According to ECFA rules, the board of directors cannot be from the same family, fund-raising tactics are regulated, and accountability is enforced. ECFA organizations are seeking to maintain a high ethical stance.

On the corporate level, ethical purity is mandatory if we are to experience the full blessing of God; George Mueller of Bristol, England, a man known for his prayers of faith and his mighty influence on others, set forth seven statements of ethical commitment. How would modern Christian organizations fare under the light of these guidelines, as quoted by Catherine Marshall in *Beyond Our Selves*?

1. No funds would ever be solicited. No facts and figures concerning needs were to be revealed by the workers in the orphanage to anyone, except to God in prayer.
2. No debts would ever be incurred.
3. No money contributed for a specific purpose would ever be used for another purpose.
4. All accounts would be audited annually by professional auditors.
5. No ego-pandering by publication of donor's names, with the amount of their gifts, would be allowed; each donor would be thanked privately.
6. No "names" of prominent or titled persons would be sought for the board or to advertise the

institution.

7. The success of the institution would be measured not by the numbers served or by the amounts of money taken in, but by God's blessing on the work, which Mueller expected to be in proportion to the time in prayer.[9]

But what about on the personal level? How do we regulate ourselves? Having friends who will hold us accountable (more on this later in the chapter) can certainly help. It can be beneficial to make other decisions such as these:

- staying as free from debt as possible;
- paying off credit cards every month (so that we do not get accustomed to living beyond our means);
- being satisfied to be a little "behind the times" with respect to all the latest possessions that advertisers tell us we *must* have;
- keeping our financial word (rather than paying people late or reneging on debts).

We live in a world of complicated personal ethics because standards have become relative. Christian leaders must strive, in business, in the home, and in the church, to be ethically above reproach with the management of money, believing that we are *stewards* of God's resources.

COMMITMENT 2: SIMPLICITY

The stewardship theme leads us to another

commitment: simplicity. As stewards of God's resources and citizens of His world, we must see the need for a simpler, more materialistically-free lifestyle. John Stott quotes Dr. John Klotz: "Science cannot find a way of spreading the standard of living of modern western man all over the globe."[10]

If Klotz is right, then there are only two choices: either western man will simplify his lifestyle so the wealth can, in effect, be spread over a broader population; or western man will continue at the acquisitional, materialist pace of the past and, in so doing, continue to live at the expense of the rest of the world. It seems that we talk about the former option, but we live according to the latter one. To simplify is a radical choice.

A commitment to a simpler lifestyle actually liberates. My wife and I have chosen to buy older, used cars. As a result, we are free from the fear of scratches or dents— not to mention from higher insurance costs. We have chosen *not* to own a VCR or to subscribe to cable television. This might sound archaic to some, but it frees us to have more time to spend with each other in more ancient traditions—like personal conversations or quiet evenings around the house!

A simpler life gives us the feeling of being a little "out of touch." A house-sitter commented after three weeks in our home, "You have the most technologically out-of-date home I have ever been in: no VCR, no cable TV, no dishwasher, no air conditioning, no computer. How do you *live* there?"

A simpler life might call us to re-evaluate our

friendships. If we spend all of our time with materialistic people, our values get worn down. Bad company corrupts good morals (1 Corinthians 15:33).

One in-law of a famous evangelist who had fallen prey to materialism summed it up this way:

> In order to be accepted by those who possess wealth and influence, one has to adopt at least some of the trappings of their lifestyle and that inevitably creates conflict. Jesus said we were to be servants, but it is hard to maintain a servant's heart when you dress better than 99 percent of the world. When you play golf with senators and vacation with heads of multimillion dollar corporations, it is difficult to identify with the widow on Social Security who faithfully supports the ministry with her ten-dollar offering each month.[11]

One final word on the choices related to the simpler life: The issue at stake is not VCRs or dishwashers, but rather an understanding of the biblical principles of *stewardship* and *sacrifice*. If we understand stewardship, we quickly realize that we do not actually own anything. All that we have belongs to the Master, and He has entrusted it to us as His managers.

If we understand sacrifice, we will ask the question, "What can I do without?" rather than "What do I need?" When we focus on increasing our generosity rather than adding to our net worth, we have begun to understand the sacrificial lifestyle.

THE CALL TO MOTIVATIONAL PURITY

Why am I aspiring to be a leader? Why do I want to live a life that others will follow? All of us must face our mixed motives, the reality of a sinful ego, and then come before God asking that He will purify us. While we will realize that we are never 100 percent pure in our motivations, we can move toward purity by submitting ourselves to the scrutiny of the Holy Spirit.

If the sexual-purity battle is against the demon of lust and the financial-purity battle is against the demon of greed, then the motivational-purity battle is against the demon of pride. Let him who thinks he stands take heed lest he fall.

The best protection against pride is service. I remember arriving home after *Decision Magazine* had asked me to write an article for them. It was a great thrill, and I was prompt to tell Christie when I got home. She listened to my excitement and was thrilled with me, but when she saw that the invitation was inflating my ego, she reminded me that the cat's litter box needed changing. In a brief moment, the great writer was reduced to the cleaner of the kitty litter. Humble service keeps us from pride.

CHALLENGED ON ALL COUNTS—NOW WHAT?

The exhortation to sexual purity is a struggle for us all. Add the challenge of financial and motivational purity, and we run the risk of becoming paralyzed, unsure of how to proceed.

Without trying to oversimplify the challenge, consider the following three action items:

Action Item 1: Confession

Admitting the great sense of need we have is always a good place to start before the merciful God. Simply stating "God of holiness, help me to grow to be pure" might put us in the right frame of mind.

Confession gives us a realistic idea of what great sinners we all are, and this again keeps us from false pride. As we evaluate our own propensity to sin, we are more likely to pray as Robert Robinson did when he wrote "Come, Thou Fount of Every Blessing,"

> Prone to wander, Lord, I feel it;
> Prone to leave the God I love.
> Here's my heart, O take and seal it;
> Seal it for Thy courts above.[12]

Action Item 2: Accountability

We need others alongside of us to help keep us in line. In the conversation I had with Gordon MacDonald in the summer of 1987, he advised me, "Make sure you are meeting with one or two other men who will ask you *tough questions* about your walk with God, your sexual control, your obedience."

We are accountable to God, our spouse, and each other. However, we live in a culture that separates us from each other. We can hide financial mis-management from nearly everyone (sometimes even our spouse). Lustful thoughts or an addiction to pornography can be pushed into a dirty corner of our lives that only God sees. To grow in purity, we must submit ourselves to others for examination, exhortation, and healing.

We can supplement our accountability to others by reading slowly through literature designed to challenge our Christian maturity. Consider, as an example, these questions related to sexual purity that I had to read carefully as I read Kent Hughes' *Liberating Ministry from the Success Syndrome*:

1. Are we being desensitized by the present evil world? Do things that once shocked us now pass us by with little notice? Have our sexual ethics slackened?
2. Where do our minds wander when we have no duties to perform?
3. What are we reading? Are there books or magazines or files in our libraries that we want no one else to see?
4. What are we renting at the local video stores? How many hours do we spend watching TV? How many adulteries did we watch last week? How many murders? How many did we watch with our children?
5. How many chapters of the Bible did we read last week?[13]

Action Item 3: FIGHT!

The challenge toward purity is ongoing, and we

cannot give up. We will stumble and fall, but we must get back up: "For though a righteous man *falls* seven times, *he rises again*" (Proverbs 24:16, emphasis mine). Get back up; dust off; and start marching again.

As we grow in the fight for moral purity, we will know our personal failings, but we will also be able to pray the prayer of my friend Pat:

> Lord, I am not what I should be.
> And I am not what You want me to be.
> I am not what I could be.
> And I am not what I'd like to be.
> But I thank You, Lord,
> For I am *not what I used to be!*[14]

Part Two

The Resources of a Leader

When we consider the resources needed to rise to the challenge of leadership, we who are young are fortunate. I estimate that more has been written on leadership, management, administration, and decision making in the past twenty years than in all of human history up to that point. We are truly information-rich.

But effectiveness in leadership depends not on the resources that are available but on the resources that we use. Those who are information-rich and experience-poor will have great difficulty as leaders.

A fictional tale is told in management seminars about a young manager who was to replace a retiring executive. The younger man approached the older, venerated leader and asked, "Sir, I know of the legend that you have become as a leader in this company. Could you give me some advice as I try to fill your shoes?"

The older man pondered the question and responded: "Three words: *Make good decisions!*"

"That is good advice," the young man replied as he

wrote this down. "And what is the key to making good decisions?"

"One word," the veteran executive replied. "*Experience.*"

"And how do I get this," the eager young man asked as he scribbled "experience" on his paper.

"Two words," the retiring man answered. "*Bad decisions.*"

The younger man looked surprised, and the older man asked, "Any other questions?"

The older man wanted the younger to know that some leadership wisdom can only be acquired through mistakes—learning by the "seat of the pants" as it is sometimes called.

But we know from the command of Paul to Timothy that youthfulness does not disqualify one from leadership. It simply puts a higher demand on that leader—to lead an exemplary life and to draw on all the resources possible to make up for inexperience.

FEELING ILL-EQUIPPED? WE'RE NOT ALONE

Biblical leaders—especially those called in their youth—were often intimidated by the challenges of leadership:

Moses, even though he was eighty years old, exhausted all of his excuses as to why he could not lead. When these did not satisfy God, he simply asked, "Please send someone else" (Exodus 3-4).

Barak was not courageous enough to lead the Israelites into battle by himself. He had to recruit the inspiring help of Deborah (Judges 4).

Gideon felt so insecure about God's call for him to lead that he tested God twice to make sure of the commission to go into battle (Judges 6).

Jeremiah reluctantly accepted his call as a young prophet, but only after he had told God that he did not know how to speak because he was so young (Jeremiah 1).

Peter certainly felt the sting of failure and inadequacy after his youthful zeal was not enough to give him courage to stand for his Lord. He probably wanted to echo Moses, saying, "Lord, You know the failure that I have been. Please send someone else."

Timothy, the recipient of Paul's exhortation to live an exemplary life in order to give credence to his ministry as a young leader, certainly knew fear, the desire to quit, and the feeling of incompetence.

By the grace of God, all of these people rose to meet their challenge as leaders. They had God's call as their motivation, and they drew on the resources that He provided for them.

TAPPING THE RESOURCES

I am not much of an outdoorsman, but I do appreciate being with people who understand the wilderness. Gerry is one of those people. As he walks through the woods of New Hampshire, he can get his bearings, direct fellow travelers to safe drinking water, and show which plants of the forest are edible.

If I were lost in the wilderness, I would want to be

with Gerry. He is not the strongest or most athletic hiker I have ever met, but he knows the forest. In the face of the challenges of being lost, he would know where to find the resources needed to keep us alive.

Gerry illustrates leadership. Leadership does not require us to be vaults of wisdom or tremendous sources of knowledge. Leadership means that we know where to turn, where to find the resources we need in the face of challenges.

As leaders, we will find ourselves lost in the woods at times. When we do, we will need to look for resources to help us along. Leaders do not have all the answers, but they know how to use other resources to get them.

Consider four resources that every leader—especially we who are young—must learn to draw upon effectively: enthusiasm, knowledge, idealism, and older leaders.

6
Enthusiasm for God

Where do we go for the energy needed to be a leader in our complicated world? What resource can we tap to help us maintain the integrity needed to endure in our challenge to live an exemplary life? And what resource will help us to endure (rather than to burn out at a young age).

The first resource available to the young leader is enthusiasm. Deriving its meaning from *en*, meaning "in," and *theos* ("God"), the word literally means to be "infused with God."

While the word enthusiasm never appears in the Bible, the idea of being "infused with God" is present throughout. Those who give their total energies in God's service are affirmed, while those who are halfhearted are spurned. To be "hot" for God is more desirable than being "lukewarm" (Revelation 3:15-16).

Paul wrote to Timothy and exhorted him several times to be full of God's power in the service he rendered as a church leader:

- Second Timothy 1:7—God has given a spirit of power, love, and self-discipline to strengthen Timothy in the face of his challenges.
- First Timothy 1:18—Paul exhorts Timothy to keep strong in fighting the good fight.
- First Timothy 4:15-16—More commands to Timothy that he be diligent, that he persevere, that he "give [himself] wholly" to the issues of leadership.
- Second Timothy 2:15—A return to the theme of diligence, applied now to the study of God's Word.

In the face of guaranteed persecution (2 Timothy 3:12), Paul wrote to push his younger partner to maintain diligence, to persevere, to be absorbed with the things of God. Timothy did not have the ability within himself to do this; he had to draw on the power of God within him. He could not be halfhearted; he had to be infused with God's Spirit.

ENTHUSIASM NEEDED

The biblical concept of being filled with God (or filled with God's Spirit, the Holy Spirit [Ephesians 5:18]) should not be reduced to simple excitement, like enthusiasm at a high school football game. The enthusiasm that we need to draw upon comes from dedicating ourselves completely to God and His purposes.

Pericles and Demosthenes were contemporaries in Greece. Both were fine speakers, but one was an orator, and the other was a motivator. When the orator spoke, people marveled at his ability to turn a phrase or argue a point. When the motivator spoke, people rose up to follow.

Enthusiasm enables us to be motivators.

ENTHUSIASM TO KNOW GOD

I met Gary at the campus of the University of Massachusetts. He had recently committed his life to Christ, and a friend asked me to start meeting with Gary to see how I could encourage his growth.

Gary had no Christian background. He had never been to church. When I first met him, I could see his excitement about his newfound faith combined with a lack of spiritual information. I knew he had to start reading the Bible, so I gave him a New Testament and instructed him to start with the Gospel of John. Two days later he called me (we were not due to meet for five more days). "What can I read now?" he asked. I pointed him to Romans.

A few days later he had finished Romans. By week one he had also completed his first reading of all the other gospels. By week two he had completed the New Testament. I found myself attracted to Gary because he was voracious in his desire to know God. His hunger for God's Word inspired me.

Gary had found a relationship with God, and he was going after it with all of his might. He made it his ambition to know and please God, imitating Paul when he wrote, "So we make it our goal to please him" (2 Corinthians 5:9).

J. C. Ryle wrote in the spiritual classic *Holiness* about the proper enthusiasm that Gary illustrated:

> Zeal in religion is a burning desire to please God, to do his will, and to advance his glory in the world in every possible way. . . . *A zealous man in religion is preeminently a man of one thing* (emphasis mine).[1]

Ryle draws from the Pauline statement "But one thing I do" in Philippians 3:13 to say that enthusiasm is manifested in our priorities. Gary wanted nothing else but to know God, and this desire captured his heart, his energy, his time. He was striving, even as a young Christian, to be a man of one thing.

Charles Spurgeon, in *Lectures to My Students*, observed that,

> In many instances, ministerial success is traceable almost entirely to an intense zeal, a consuming passion for souls, and an eager enthusiasm in the cause of God, and we believe that in every case, other things being equal, men prosper in the divine service in proportion as their hearts are blazing with holy love.[2]

As we continue in our walk with Christ, our zeal sometimes wanes and our fervor dissipates. Let us pray the prayer of the psalmist that we might return to be people of one thing:

> Teach me your way O LORD,
> and I will walk in your truth;

give me an undivided heart,
that I may fear your name. (Psalm 86:11, emphasis mine)

ENTHUSIASM TO RELATE GOD'S WORD TO OUR WORLD

The basic theme of John Stott's book on preaching, *Between Two Worlds*, is that good preaching addresses both the world of the Bible and the modern world. The effective preacher is zealous to apply the truths of Scripture to the contemporary culture.

Paul exemplified this zeal in 1 Corinthians 9:16-17 as he described his own compulsion to preach the gospel. He lived with a sense of being an ambassador of Christ (2 Corinthians 5:20), earnestly desiring to see all of his listeners reconciled to God through the gospel of Jesus Christ. He was enthusiastic that his world would understand the Word.

Enthusiasm for applying the Word of God to the world is contagious. When we get excited about the relevancy of the Scriptures in our times, fellow Christians join with us. John White reminds us in *Excellence in Leadership* that "people do not follow programs, but leaders who inspire them. They act when a vision stirs them in a reckless hope of something greater than themselves, hope of fulfillment they had never before dared to aspire to."[3]

Leadership means getting excited about applying God's Word to our world. As we grow in our focused zeal for God, we will attract others to join with us.

Enthusiasm to See God's Changes

When we pray, "Thy Kingdom come," we ask God to bring about change in our world. When we live by the power of God and earnestly desire to see those changes, we begin to experience biblical enthusiasm.

"Thy-will-be-done" enthusiasm is not lighthearted positive thinking that naively says, "If we can think it, we can do it," like the little engine who made it up the hill just by chanting, "I think I can; I think I can."

"Thy-will-be-done" enthusiasm understands that we cannot do it on our own—we must rely on the transforming, supernatural power of God. But we are not melancholy or hopeless. No pessimist ever made a great leader. With "Thy-will-be-done" enthusiasm, we can properly look optimistically at every difficulty, realizing that God can use it for good.

John Stott calls for leaders with this type of enthusiasm in *Involvement*: "Nothing much happens without a dream. And for something great to happen, there must be great dreams. Behind every achievement is a dreamer of great dreams."[4]

When we are seeking God's Kingdom, we can be excited to dream dreams of the changes He will make through our obedience.

Enthusiastic to Believe God for His Work in Others

We consider Bob's commitment to Christ one of the most exciting events in our lives. Christie had been witnessing to Bob, her brother, for over ten years, but we seldom saw any spiritual hunger in him. He seemed happy with his life, and he saw no need for anything other than a peripheral commitment to religion.

Then God started to answer her prayers. Bob expressed a desire to come to church, to read the Bible, to ask questions about the faith. Christie would spend hours on the phone with him, helping him to understand a personal commitment to Jesus Christ.

Finally, after one particular marathon discussion, Christie asked Bob, "Does all of this make sense to you?"

"Yes," he replied.

"Would you like to receive Christ now?" Christie asked.

"Yes, I would," Bob answered, and Christie led him in prayer as he committed his life to Christ. Her prayer of years was answered! God had done the greatest possible work in Bob's life. We found it hard to believe, ourselves, but God had done it.

Paul the apostle lived a life of enthusiastic support for what God could do in the lives of others. He told the Colossians that he desired to see them complete in Christ (Colossians 1:28), and he affirmed to the Philippians that God would complete the good work that He had started in them (Philippians 1:6). Paul's understudy, Timothy, received the maximum encouragement from him, who enthusiastically saw the man of God that Timothy could become (see 1 Timothy 6:11-21). Paul demonstrates excitement about what God wants to do in the lives of others.

WHAT ENTHUSIASM IS NOT

Enthusiasm, according to our "infused with God" definition, is not reserved for young leaders only, but the energy of youth makes us uniquely capable of drawing on enthusiasm to the utmost.

We must be aware, however, of some of the potential abuses of zeal in leadership.

Enthusiasm Is Not Obsession

The American workaholic can use enthusiasm as an excuse for never taking a rest. In our achievement-oriented culture, obsessive-compulsive drives can actually draw us away from God rather than toward Him.

In the book *The Tyranny of Time*, Robert Banks traces some of our cultural obsessions with productivity to our Anglo-Saxon roots. He points out, for example, that the Spanish word for a clock's movement means "walks," whereas an English clock "runs."[5] He goes on to show how this simple distinction has influenced an entire culture to be obsessed with the demon of busyness. Banks writes about obsessive activity in our culture:

> The going itself, movement for its own sake, has taken the place of more fundamental questions about who they are and where they are heading. Those who are caught up in the busy life have neither the time nor quiet to come to understand themselves and their goals.[6]

Christian leaders who are overloaded with responsibilities or commitments are not demonstrating an enthusiasm for God and His Kingdom. They are simply revealing that they are caught in the compulsive drive of modern life that leads to what Paul Tournier calls "universal fatigue."[7]

Enthusiasm Is Not Control

Some leaders claim great zeal for God and demonstrate it by trying to gain control over the lives of others. In a misguided desire to lead, these leaders weave zeal together with a tendency to manipulate others.

Pastor Frank's zeal for God got corrupted somewhere along the trail. His strong walk with Christ gave him a zeal and confidence that attracted people to him. His ministry grew, and many came to him for answers to their problems. Unfortunately, Pastor Frank's zeal gradually mutated into a desire to control the people that were coming to him. He became irate when anyone questioned his word; he excommunicated any who did not accept him as God's authority. His zeal degenerated; now he is the pastor of a small independent church that he founded, and he tries to control the thirty-five people who vow allegiance to him.

ENTHUSIASM AND COMMITMENT

Soren Kierkegaard wrote that "purity of heart is to will one thing."[8] This is where enthusiasm is rooted—

to will one thing, to be a person with a demonstrated commitment to seek to know Christ above all else.

Enthusiasm cannot be separated from other disciplines discussed in this book, such as study, prayer, or obedience. We must have both the *heat* of enthusiasm and the *light* of the Scriptures.

D. Martyn Lloyd-Jones relates a humorous story about this combined commitment in *Preaching and Preachers:*

> There was an old preacher whom I knew very well in Wales. He was a very able old man and a good theologian; but, I'm sorry to say, he had a tendency towards cynicism. But he was a very able critic. On one occasion he was present at a synod in the final session of which two men were preaching. Both these men were professors of theology. The first man preached, and when he had finished, this old preacher, this old critic, turned to his neighbor and said, "Light without heat." Then the second professor preached —he was an older man and somewhat emotional. When he had finished the old cynic turned to his neighbor and said, "Heat without light." He was right in both cases.[9]

Finding the balance between proper enthusiasm and a commitment to the "light" underscores the need for a commitment to *take time to think*. We must never be so overcome with enthusiasm that we proceed blindly or without thought. "The less opportunity there is to think," writes Banks in *The Tyranny of Time*, "the less likelihood we will form sound judgments. The less sound judgments we make, the less adequate decisions we will make."[10]

Enthusiasm for God likewise implies that we are willing to "die daily" for Kingdom-of-God causes—whether that be service to the needy or finding Jesus in the mundane aspects of life ("practicing the presence of God," as Brother Lawrence calls it).[11] Enthusiasm is not just emotion; it is the dogged endurance required to persevere in the face of obstacles, to get up when we fall, to work hard for higher purposes.

CONCLUSION

The energy of our younger years must be committed to Jesus Christ so that we are infused with His power. Our energies will fail, but He can keep us going. The first resource that we must tap is enthusiasm as we seek to be filled with the Holy Spirit as young leaders.

General Dwight D. Eisenhower illustrated enthusiasm in leadership by laying a foot-long piece of string on the table before him. "If I push this string," he'd say, "it really gets nowhere, for it bunches up on itself. But if I pull the string, it will follow me wherever I go." He would then conclude the object lesson by challenging his associates to be zealous leaders that others would follow.

Enthusiasm—use it wisely, and put it into practice.

People are waiting to follow young men and women who are totally enthusiastic for God and His purposes.

7
Applying Your Knowledge

We are information-rich. The people of Old Testament times might have perished for lack of knowledge (Hosea 4:6), but we are in no such danger. We've had a knowledge explosion. The knowledge and information available to us serve as tremendous resources to those who aspire to leadership.

But knowledge is both a blessing and a curse. Two hundred years ago, people in New York would not find out about an earthquake in Asia for weeks—if they ever heard about it! Because of modern technology, we know about earthquakes anywhere in the world as *they are happening*! We are privy to so much knowledge that we can echo the words of Solomon in Ecclesiastes, "For with much wisdom comes much sorrow; the more knowledge, the more grief" (1:18).

We might sarcastically respond, "Ignorance is bliss!" It seems easier at times to stay ignorant than to seek knowledge. The amount of information available to us can overwhelm us with the plea, "What can I do in response to all this?"

Adolphe Monod said, "Between the great things we

cannot do and the small things we will not do, the danger is that we shall do nothing."[1] Information overload can lead to inactivity, mental paralysis, or even apathy.

But knowledge is a resource that we can learn to manage well as we aspire to grow as leaders. We will never be able to respond to all that we learn, but we have the privilege of learning in broader and deeper ways than many who have gone before us.

EFFECTIVE LEADERS NEED KNOWLEDGE

Effectiveness in leadership relates directly to the discipline of learning and the management of knowledge. A disciple of Jesus Christ is fundamentally a learner, one who is constantly growing. Jesus commands us to follow Him and to learn from Him (Matthew 11:29).

We Need Knowledge of the Bible

When I went to a seminary bookstore one day, I noted that one complete wall was filled with shelves of commentaries on the Bible. Thousands, if not millions, of hours of scholarly research lay in the pages of the books on that wall, and they were available to me.

A wall filled with commentaries might not be the secret to knowledge of the Bible (for many have technical biblical knowledge without love of Christ), but the books reminded me that we in the English-speaking world have no excuse for ignorance about God's Word. The written resources, various translations, and multiple commentaries represent a vast ocean of knowledge available to us all.

But, in reality, it seems that people are not reading as zealously as publishers are publishing. However, if people are not reading new books, at least they are reading the Bible, right? Not necessarily. More people may be reading the Bible's essential texts through devotional guides or condensations such as the *Reader's Digest Bible*, but who is *studying* the Bible? Reading only favorite parts of the Scriptures may show our unwillingness to be stretched or to study the more "boring" texts, seeking a quicker "blessing."

Writer Amos Wells reflected our need for thorough Bible study in this verse:

I supposed I knew my Bible,
  Reading piecemeal, hit or miss,
Now a bit of John or Matthew,
  Now a snatch of Genesis,
Certain chapters of Isaiah,
  Certain Psalms (the twenty-third),
Twelfth of Romans, first of Proverbs —
  Yes, I thought I new the Word!
But I found that thorough reading
  Was a different thing to do,
And the way was unfamiliar
  When I read the Bible through.
You who like to play at Bible,
  Dip and dabble, here and there,
Just before you kneel, aweary,
  And yawn through a hurried prayer;

You who treat the Crown of Writings
    As you treat no other book,
Just a paragraph, disjointed,
    Just a crude, impatient look,
Try a worthier procedure,
    Try a broad and steady view;
You will kneel in very rapture
    When you read the Bible through.[2]

If we are learners, we must tackle the Scriptures in total. The selective reading of our favorite texts must be secondary to the disciplined reading and studying of the whole. Utilizing the vast resource of scriptural knowledge requires us to recommit ourselves to believe the verse that tells us all Scripture is inspired by God and is profitable to equip the man or woman of God (2 Timothy 3:16).

"Oh, how I love your law," the psalmist exclaimed. "I meditate on it all day long" (Psalm 119:97). Resourceful leaders make this verse their prayer and practice, realizing that their first call is to grow in grace and in the knowledge of the Lord (2 Peter 3:18).

We Need Knowledge of Ourselves

Tremendous learning is available to the person who follows the Socratic mandate to "know thyself." In an age of self-discovery, self-actualization, and self-acceptance, however, the reading of oneself can be misconstrued as an act of selfishness, the very antithesis of the servanthood demanded of Christian leaders.

On the contrary, knowing oneself is a resource

because it gives us a deeper understanding of the grace and mercy of God at work in our lives. Through the scrutiny of the Scriptures (Psalm 139, for example) and the help of others (Proverbs 27:5-6,17), we can begin to understand life, patterns, habits, personal strengths and weaknesses, and even our own personalities in an effort to grow.

Self-knowledge does not require a monastic life, but it does demand time for proper introspection (or self-examination). In the face of success or failure, solitude or fellowship, we grow through evaluating what motivates us, how we respond, and where we most need God to help us grow.

Personally, the discipline of writing in a journal has been my most valuable tool for self-knowledge and an understanding of the person God has made me. In the journal, I can trace the hand of God in my life and my progress toward (or regress from) Christlike attitudes and behavior.

The first purpose of the personal, spiritual journal is *to remember*. The psalmist tells us, "I will remember the deeds of the LORD" (Psalm 77:11). My journal entries help me remember that God will work through me, weak as I am.

The second function of the journal is *to articulate*. Without time set aside to think and write, I am apt to live without a sense of discernment of what God is doing in my life. In light of my fluctuating emotions and experiences, the recording of my daily pilgrimage helps me see how God is sovereignly orchestrating my life.

The third purpose of the journal is *to meditate.* Writing out prayers, copying Scripture texts, recording key spiritual quotations, and writing my responses all contribute to my spiritual growth. Without the discipline of writing, my mind races ahead to the activities of the day and militates against my meditating or thinking deeply.

We Need Knowledge of People

Knowing ourselves is complemented by our growth in knowing others. Effectiveness in leadership depends, in part, on our ability to understand what makes other people tick—what their needs are, and how we can help them grow.

Jesus was able to affect the multitudes because He could "read" them; He saw their faces, perhaps their clothing or their body language, and He perceived that they were harassed and helpless, like sheep without a shepherd (Mark 6:34).

While we will never have the full insight of the Lord, I doubt that the people Jesus saw were much different from those we see every day in traffic jams, in shopping lines, or at our places of employment. The difference is that Jesus was spiritually alert to their frustrations, fears, and hurts.

Through observation of others, counseling, and reading, we can develop our ability to read people. The unspoken needs, the fears and frustrations, and the pains of people around us are readily readable if we stop and look.

When people come into our fellowships as visitors

and leave with the feeling, "No one cared about me," perhaps it is because we are too busy in "ministry" to stop and read people. If we take the time to develop our knowledge of people, God will give us the wisdom we need to read their needs and care for them.

We Need Knowledge of Our World

In the rapid pace of our daily lives, we often forget to study the world around us. We may have more books than ever before, but we often lack the power of observation.

The world around us includes nature. The psalmist says, "The heavens declare the glory of God; the skies proclaim the work of his hands" (Psalm 19:1). As we contemplate the marvels of God's creation, our view of God and our standing in the world grows. God—who even calls every star by name (Isaiah 40:26)—chooses to use us. Gaze up into the night sky and think about that!

Reading nature is a wonderful discipline because it withstands our deepest research and discovery. Few of us are incapable of experiencing the beauty of a sunset, the fragrance of flowers, or the melody of the songbird. Acquiring knowledge includes searching everything for "the fingerprint of God," as Joseph Bayly exhorted.[3] God has surrounded us with His "fingerprints" if we only take time to observe.

The world around us includes our culture and our times. Christians who react to the harsh news of the world by swearing off newspapers will have a difficult time applying the Word to the world. Half of the necessary knowledge for relevance will be lacking.

But, as we observed earlier, great knowledge yields great sorrow. Christie works in a microbiology lab where they examine various specimens from AIDS patients. As a result, the hospital tries to keep health workers aware of the on-going research. In a lab briefing, AIDS researchers told of the sexual lifestyle of homosexuals who made themselves most susceptible to contracting AIDS. The reports both horrified and saddened Christie because of the depth of immorality into which some had sunk. It would have been easier not to know.

Leighton Ford, in an excerpt from Engstrom's *Seizing the Torch*, reflected these challenges back in the 1980's as he confronted leaders with the world ahead:

> It will be a *larger* world. If you are 50, the world has doubled in your lifetime. By the year 2000 there will be one and one-half billion more people. India will be the biggest country with more than all of Africa and Latin America.
>
> It will be a *developing* world. Eighty percent of the population will be in developing countries by 2025. Sixty percent will be in Asia.
>
> It will be an *older* world. By 2025 there will be one billion people over 60—one in every 7.
>
> It will also be a *younger* world.

Sixty percent are now under 24. Half of Latin America is under 18. Mexico City has a population under 14 equal to New York City. There is not a Third World city with a median age over 20.

It will be an *urban* world. Mexico City will have 31 million by the year 2000. By 2000 there will be 22 mega cities, with ten million plus.

It will certainly be a world of *conflict*. Fifty percent of our scientific minds are engaged in so-called "defense." Many fully expect a nuclear terrorist incident or one between the new nuclear nations by 2000.

It will be the world of the "*information era*." A world divided not between the haves and have-nots, but between knows and know-nots. We can now send the Encyclopedia Brittanica across the Atlantic six times a minute. If the auto industry kept up with computer information advance, a Rolls-Royce would get 3 million miles a gallon, would cost less than $3 and you could put six on the head of a pin. Jean Pierre du Prie, an information specialist, said "The more we 'communicate' the way we do, the more we create a hellish world. Ours is a world about which we pretend to have more information, yet one that is increasingly

> void of meaning."
>
> And it will be a different world in religion. Islam is growing 16 percent a year; Hinduism is growing 12 percent, Buddhism 10 percent, Christianity 9 percent. There are now more Muslims than Baptists in Britain. Yet David Barrett speaks of the era of "universal response" and "global access."[4]

Ford wrote these words over twenty years ago, but the challenges he reflects face us today more than ever. Ours is an incredibly challenging world, and we must fully tap the knowledge available to us to be as effective as possible in leading the Church and bringing the gospel to this world.

KNOWLEDGE MUST BE PUT TO WORK

To serve as a resource, the knowledge we have access to must be put to work. Without application, knowledge is useless.

We Must Commit Ourselves to the Process of Growth

Remember again Jesus' command: "Take my yoke upon you and learn from me" (Matthew 11:29). Knowledge is not acquired simply through academic degrees or intellectual development; knowledge is part of the ongoing commitment of discipleship.

We Must Act on What We Know

We must be doers of the Word (James 1:22), not merely reserves where knowledge is stored. Loving Jesus means not only knowing His Word or His commands; we must obey (John 14:21,23). Better is a little knowledge with application than a library full of unused facts.

We Must Prioritize Our Learning

We are confronted with a vast ocean of knowledge, but we cannot possibly take it all in. We must look over this vast ocean, and then, by God's grace, decide where He wants us to dive in. We cannot be dedicated to vain intellectual development nor to "trivial pursuit." We have to personally determine before God what (in addition to knowledge of His will through the Scriptures) our priorities should be: Science? Religion? Family life? AIDS? Government relations? Business? Whatever our vocational calling from God, we must tap the knowledge available to be as effective as possible as Christian leaders in these fields.

We Must Manage Our Knowledge with Humility

Knowledge puffs up; love edifies (1 Corinthians 8:1). Without proper humility, we will become like the fool in Proverbs who delights not in understanding but only in revealing his own mind (Proverbs 18:2). We are servants of Christ, and knowledge is our servant. P.T. Forsyth wrote in 1907 that the need of the hour was for an "authoritative gospel in a humble personality."[5] The need remains today.

We Must Use Our Knowledge Evangelistically

In the December 1986 issue of *World Evangelization*, the leaders of the Lausanne Committee issued a ten-point challenge, the second of which was, "The challenge of using technology to reach the world."[6] We can never forget that God's goal is that the earth will be full of the knowledge of the Lord as the waters cover the sea (Isaiah 11:9) and that He cares primarily that people are saved and come to a knowledge of the truth (1 Timothy 2:4). With ninety-eight percent of the unreached peoples outside North America and approximately eighty-five percent of these in areas where no immediate Christian witness exists, "someone has to cross cultural, linguistic, and political frontiers to get to them. They will not come to us and ask for something of which they have never heard."[7] We must use the knowledge to which we have access to get the Word out.

KNOWLEDGE ACQUISITION—SOME PRACTICAL STEPS

As we struggle to use the resource of knowledge in the most efficient ways possible, some practical ideas might be helpful:

Idea 1: Find a System that Works for You

Our ability to use knowledge as a resource will depend to some extent on our ability to retrieve what we have learned. Note cards, files, notebooks, computers, or memory are all part of this retrieval process. Find the best systems that work for you, and develop them.

Idea 2: Develop the Ability to Find Answers

Resourcefulness is not having all the answers but knowing where to look for them. Know how to use libraries. Draw on the research of others. When looking for a specific answer, use indexes in books rather than reading the entire text.

Idea 3: Use Knowledge Management Resources

Newsletters are valuable in summarizing many facts or events succinctly. Computer technology, when available, can be a valuable asset. If there is the possibility of gaining an administrative assistant in your field of specialization, work with him or her to manage information flow.

Idea 4: Make Learning a Team Effort

If you work in a team setting, spread the learning around and then share your findings. Some families find it entertaining to delegate specialties to various family members. One resourceful pastor recruited a reading team from his church so that he could draw upon a broader base of research for his sermons and sermon illustrations.

Idea 5: Set Learning Goals

With the amount of information we are required to manage daily, we may never find time to learn anything new. Learning a foreign language, developing a mind-enriching hobby, or even reading for enjoyment may never occur unless we set personal goals.

CONCLUSION

We are looking out across the vast horizon called knowledge, and as we seek to be leaders of others, we proceed forward with caution, using knowledge as a resource to help us, but never forgetting that if we can "fathom all mysteries and all knowledge . . . but have not love, [we are] nothing" (1 Corinthians 13:2).

8
The Right Kind of Idealism

We can make a difference!

The cynic and the pessimist doubt that statement, but as people of faith, we believe it. Our idealism, especially when we are young, is built not on naive positive thinking or trust in our own abilities but rather on God who delights in using the weak things of the world for His purposes (1 Corinthians 1:26-31).

Vision and faith should be part of our "standard operating procedure" as young leaders. However, we can fall prey to the attacks of pessimism. In light of the overwhelming challenges we face—both in the development of our inner character and in response to our needy world—we might doubt that we make any difference at all.

We are part of a generation that Arthur Levine described in the book *When Dreams and Heroes Died*. He evaluated ours as a culture where many no longer believe that they can make a difference. Dreams—and the heroes that personified those dreams—have died, leaving young people with bitterness, fear, or hostility toward the future.[1]

In contrast, John Stott calls leaders to repent of this pessimism because it is "dishonouring to God and incompatible with Christian faith."[2] Stuart Briscoe, in *David: A Heart for God*, urges leaders to realize that although cynics are present everywhere, even in the Christian Church, we cannot be cynical. "When it comes to spiritual fruit in your life," Briscoe wrote, "healthy productivity will never spring up out of a heart cynical towards God and His people. I urge you to put away the very last trace of cynicism from your heart and life."[3]

The forward progress of the Christian Church depends on leaders who have renounced cynicism and replaced it with healthy biblical idealism. We need to regain biblical dreams about what God wants to do through His Church in the world. In the words of the late Robert E. Kennedy, we need to stop seeing things the way they are and saying "Why?" and start dreaming of the way things could be and saying "Why not?"

I work at a church that is the product of people's faith and idealism. In the 1960s, when New England was called "the graveyard of preachers" or "the rockiest spiritual soil in America," God raised up lay men and women who believed that He could do a great work in the greater Boston area. Others have come alongside the founding members over these past years, caught the vision of faith, and the church has grown—both quantitatively and qualitatively. One of the reasons for the consistent growth has been leaders who chose to believe God rather than the cynics who said, "Spiritual and numerical growth cannot happen in New England."

We need leaders with vision, leaders who see opportunities rather than obstacles, who will stand against pessimists who utter the seven last words of the church—"we never did it that way before"—leaders who want to be part of the fulfillment of Joel's prophecy of dreaming dreams and seeing visions (Joel 2:28, Acts 2:17).

At the LEADERSHIP 88 conference for younger leaders, Luis Palau called men and woman to the following four commitments:

- Commitment to unquenchable optimism.
- Commitment to unwavering success (in terms of obedience to God).
- Commitment to unforgettable influence (leaving the "aroma of Christ" wherever we go).
- Commitment to unimpeachable integrity.

We are called to idealistic, biblical leadership—unquenchable optimism—and not the second-class Christianity for which many seem to settle. A.W. Tozer reflected on the deep problems in the church of his day (and perhaps of our day as well):

> Personally, I have for years carried a burden of sorrow as I have moved among evangelical Christians who somewhere in their past have managed to strike a base compromise with their heart's holier longings and settled down to a lukewarm,

> mediocre kind of Christianity utterly unworthy of themselves and of the Lord they claim to serve.[4]

BUILDING BIBLICAL IDEALISM

The Bible calls us to be people of faith. As such, we are not blind to the brokenness of our world nor to the challenges before us. We have a realistic optimism and the belief that God uses us to bring about positive change.

Growing in this ability to make a difference, however, requires *commitment*, something many young men and women shy away from. In a book describing the young adult generation, Susan Littwin observes that young adults

> would like to achieve and have influence and recognition, but they are unwilling to take the risk. They talk a lot about freedom and adventure, which often turn out to be code words for not making a commitment. For as long as they haven't made a commitment, their illusions about life remain unchanged. Caught between their sense of entitlement and their fear of failure, they live in a fantasyland of infinite choices.[5]

Idealism without commitment, Littwin says, leaves one living in a fantasy world thinking, "I can do whatever

I'd like," when in reality he or she does nothing because of the fear of making commitments. This idealism, while believing that there are "limitless choices, arrayed like cereals on the market shelves," fears commitment because it requires dedication to one task and the necessary elimination of others. The person who desires to keep all options open will never make a significant impact anywhere.[6]

The value of our dreams—our idealism—will depend on our ability to bring them into reality through commitments. Leadership with dreams and no commitment will launch us into a fantasy world where we are chasing after windmills in imaginary battles, like Don Quixote.

Commitment 1: Start Where We Are

Where can we start making a difference now? What abilities, skills, and resources do we have to offer right where we are? And what opportunities has God given us to start dreaming His dreams?

Developing our Christian idealism—a belief that God wants to use us to make a difference—starts with a healthy "reality quotient." That is, we start with a realistic appraisal of who we are, what we have to offer, and where God has put us. The "reality quotient" helps us dedicate ourselves afresh to the commitment of being *excellent* rather than *successful.* Success focuses on making a difference that outshines the achievements of others. Excellence focuses on making the greatest difference I can with the unique abilities God has given me. "*Success* bases our worth on comparison to others. *Excellence* gauges our value by measuring us against our own potential."[7]

A group at our church meets regularly to discuss future cross-cultural ministry. This "Potential Missionary Fellowship" shares dreams about making a difference in the work of the gospel around the world. But our "reality quotient" tells us that God has placed us here for now—so how will we start making a difference?

Several members started reaching out to international students. Others are seeking to evangelize coworkers, neighbors, and fellow students. A member of this group led her father to Christ as she sought to make a difference where God had placed her now.

Commitment 2: Take Educated Risks of Faith

Faith and idealism, like muscles, need to be exercised. We grow as leaders when we step out and take risks before God. Fred Smith laments that "too many congregations have no purpose larger than to be an *average* church doing *average* things. That doesn't require great leadership. It requires what I call 'maintenance leadership.' It's not building for the future" (emphasis mine).[8]

The only remedy for our addiction to averageness is to step out in faith. Try something never tried before. Ask God for new dreams! Take risks in witnessing, leading, and teaching, and see how God stretches our faith!

Hudson Taylor, the great man of faith who founded the China Inland Mission, integrated faith and risk. He said, "Unless there is an element of risk in our exploits for God, there is no need for faith."[9]

On the center of my desk, I have a plaque that simply says, "Go for it!" Some think it is unbiblical to encourage people to "go for it," but I reply, "What are the alternatives? To sit still and wait for God to push us out of our seats into action does not seem too inspirational." We need to follow the examples of people of faith—like David with Goliath or Nehemiah with his well-restoration project—and trust God and go for it.

Before God, we need to have that go-for-it spirit, willing to say, "Yes, Lord, I will step out in faith for You!"

John Stott challenges us all at the conclusion of *Involvement*:

> Don't be content with the mediocre! Don't settle for anything less than your full God-given potential! Be ambitious and adventurous for God! God has made you a unique person by your genetic endowment, upbringing, and education. He himself has created you and gifted you, and he does not want his work to be wasted. He means you to be fulfilled, not frustrated. His purpose is that everything you have and are should be stretched in his service and in the service of others.[10]

Too many of us are content to let others live lives of adventure while we watch. We applaud while Sylvester

Stallone, Mel Gibson, or Harrison Ford take great risks on the movie or television screen, but we make our choices based on security and safety. Applying Christian idealism means commitment to taking risks personally rather than living vicariously through other risk-takers.

Let's take the risk! Let's step out in faith! Let God fill us with dreams of how He wants to use us! Go for it!

Commitment 3: Teamwork

Developing the resource of idealism depends partly on our ability to motivate others to join us in fulfilling God's vision.

One of the greatest faith/idealism building exercises we have undertaken is the sending of missions work teams throughout the world. One team installed electric poles in Zambia, bringing electricity and light to the students of Manna Bible Institute. Another built a Bible school building for the churches of Burkina Faso. Painting projects in Colombia, street ministry in Manila, vacation Bible school in the Middle East, and evangelism in Montreal have stretched people's faith, teaching them that God will use their lives—together!

The dynamic growth in the participants of these work teams has been a result of their willingness to step out in faith. They have taken risks, attempted tasks, and gone places they never would have gone without the team partnership.

Teamwork goes hand in hand with humility, for teamwork changes the dream from "what God will do through *me*" to "what God will do through us." When we make that transition, we will be delighted to see God work to bless *His* work. Ted Engstrom writes, "There's no end to what you can accomplish if you don't care who gets the credit."[11] We might add, "And if you care only that God gets the glory."

Teamwork also goes with discipleship. If we have biblical "dreams" that are bigger than anything we could accomplish by ourselves, we will want to recruit others to join alongside us. Dawson Trotman, founder of The Navigators, said we must "find a man who wants God's best for his life and who is willing to pay the price to have it."[12]

The greatest works of God will be done through teams of Christian leaders who believe God for what He wants to do through them, and then are willing to make the sacrifices needed to accomplish those visions of faith.

Commitment 4: Count the Cost

The talented young people that Susan Littwin studied were lost in a fantasy because they felt entitled to success without the hard work, tough choices, or strenuous commitments that success entails.

The Christian leader realizes that there is no room for a "sense of entitlement" before God. Neither the world nor God "owes" us anything. The world is not "strung with safety nets" to catch us when we fall.[13] God will be there always, but He may allow us to learn and grow through failure as well as success.

The costs of being used by God may be more than

we expect. Jim Elliot made himself totally available to God and was killed by the Auca Indians in Ecuador while in his twenties. He has had great influence on the lives of many through his biography, *Shadow of the Almighty.*[14] Many have entered cross-cultural ministry because they were inspired by Jim Elliot. But the cost of that influence was his life.

Oswald Sanders made himself totally available to God. And he has likewise influenced many for Christ, but it has cost him thousands of hours of study, thousands of miles traveled, the harsh rebukes of his critics, and the loneliness inevitably caused by dynamic leadership. At the time of first publication of this book, he was eighty-six years old, speaking publicly almost 300 times per year, and was working on several new book ideas. His commitment to the lordship of Christ has cost him his life as well.

Mark Hatfield, a senator from Oregon, writes to challenge us to pay the price of excellence: "Each of us has a program to execute. Let us do it in such a superb manner that people will never equate mediocrity with the things of Christ."[15]

Let us be known as those who were willing to pay the price to be all that God intended for us!

Commitment 5: Perseverance

The problem with the "postponed generation" syndrome is not lack of potential but lack of perseverance. We have our dreams and our idealism, but we quit too soon, especially if the first results of our efforts are disappointing.

Consider the example of Adoniram Judson, pioneer missionary to Burma (now Myanmar). Judson and his wife, Nancy Hasseltine Judson, went out as two of the first North American missionaries, sailing in 1812 from Massachusetts. Theirs is a story of perseverance, especially in the face of great suffering.

The years in Burma were filled anguish and struggles. Learning the language of the Burmese was difficult in a country where no English was spoken; it was after more than six years of labor that they finally saw their first Christian convert, Maung Nau in 1819.

They witnessed the torture of young Burmese Christians by the government and Judson, himself, endured a torturous stint in the "Death Prison," which included being hung every night upside down in leg-irons as well as a "death march" that nearly killed him.

After his wife died Judson suffered severe depression; he sat by her grave for months, writing, "God to me is the Great Unknown; I believe in Him, but I cannot find Him."

These struggles and many more, including the personal grief of losing seven Judson children, two Judson wives, and over a dozen Judson co-workers are detailed in the account of Judson's life in *To The Golden Shore* (Courtney Anderson, 1987 (Judson Press)).

Judson devoted his life to one primary task: to give the Burmese a Bible in their own language. Judson himself died in obscurity, leaving only few converts—just a few more that a dozen.

But the mission had been completed. The Burmese had the Bible in their own language.

In a meeting several years ago with youth and youth leaders, my wife and I were scanning a copy of the Burmese Bible. The Burmese script was completely unintelligible to us, but we noticed one English sentence on the title page: "Translated by the Reverend A. Judson."

A Bible translation that had stood the test of time—over 140 years! A testimony to Judson's scholarship and meticulous linguistic study.... and ENDURANCE!

I took the Bible over to Matthew Hla Win, our host and then head of the Evangelical Fellowship. "Matthew," I asked, pointing to the English sentence,

"Do you know who this man is—Judson?"

"O yes!" he exclaimed. "Whenever someone mentions the name 'Judson' great tears come to my eyes because we know what he and his family suffered for us."

He went on with great emotion, "Today, there are over 2 million Christians in Myanmar, and every one of us trace our spiritual heritage to one man—the Reverend Adoniram Judson."

Adoniram Judson—endurance personified!

CONCLUSION

Idealism before God is a resource for young leaders, because by faith *we can act believing that we can make a difference in our broken world.* Our idealism helps us dream dreams of how God can use us—individually and together—to be His salt and light on the earth.

Go for it!

9
More Experienced Leaders

In Western culture, we are acutely aware of our resources in knowledge or technology, but we sometimes overlook what is perhaps our greatest bastion of wisdom—older leaders who have gone before us. Unlike many of the more ancient cultures of our world, we tend to honor youth and disdain the aged. Bill Cosby observes that "American culture is still a youth culture, and, like a golf tournament, we honor only the low scores."[1] Rather than seeing older people as our most valued treasure, we give preference to the young.

The writer of Proverbs exhorted his readers to listen to the words of counsel from older, more experienced people because these words were written to give "knowledge and discretion to the young" (Proverbs 1:4). To the reader who would seek wisdom in the book of Proverbs, the writer gave the promise that "you will understand what is right and just and fair—every good path. For wisdom will enter your heart, and knowledge will be pleasant to your soul. Discretion will protect you, and understanding will guard you" (Proverbs 2:9-11).

Older leaders have acquired experience, know how, and insights into life from which we may benefit. "Forty years ago we had a common cause for missionary zeal, but little leadership experience," Ted Engstrom writes. "Today we seem to lack shared purpose and cause, but are enriched with four decades of leadership experience for Christ."[2]

TAPPING THE RESOURCE

A friend had a pet cat that enjoyed being outdoors, but when the cat was ready to re-enter the house, he would scratch at the outside door. If the scratch did not achieve its desired results, then he would take two steps back and leap onto the screen door, meowing and dangling there until someone would let him in.

If we want to tap the resource of older leaders, we need the persistence of that cat. We need to let our desire to learn be known and be willing to "hang on the screen door" until someone gives us the attention we need or want.

The Bible illustrates older leaders who took the initiative toward younger men and women:

- Jethro toward Moses—Exodus 18,
- The writer of Proverbs toward his readers,
- The psalmist toward his readers—Psalm 37,
- Jesus Christ toward His disciples—Matthew 4,
- Paul toward Timothy,
- Peter toward John Mark.

But for many of us, as younger leaders, there are no older leaders coming after us to teach us. Perhaps they are just too busy. Maybe they think we will not listen to their advice. Or it could be that we seem too preoccupied with ourselves.

Whatever the reason, we, as younger leaders, need to take some initiative and go after older men and women who can teach, advise, and exhort us. If we fail to utilize this resource of older leaders, years of experience of Christian leadership in our contemporary world will be lost.

LEARN FROM THEIR EXAMPLES

"Remember your leaders, who spoke the word of God to you," writes the author of Hebrews. "Consider the outcome of their way of life and imitate their faith" (Hebrews 13:7). Older leaders have endured longer, and as a result; often bear deeper resemblance to Christ. As we look at their lives, we can "consider the outcome" of years of obedience and then follow.

Consider the Outcome: Humility

In our desire to make a difference in our world as Christian leaders, we can easily mix in personal motives for greatness or fame. The exact opposite of self-ambition is humility—a word derived from *humus*, meaning "close to the earth." In order to develop a lowly spirit, we need to study the lives of older leaders who set before us an example of humility.

Soren Kierkegaard describes a man or woman after God's own heart as one who is "early selected and slowly educated for the job."[3] Moses was such a man. He was God's chosen instrument for the release of Israel, but he learned humility *before* God made him a great leader. Forty years of wilderness experience prepared him to lead.

Kosuke Koyama writes in *The Three Mile An Hour God* that God works at the speed at which a person walks. While we would like things to happen in a hurry, God works at a pace we might find painstakingly slow. Speaking of the wanderings of the people of Israel, Koyama writes:

> Forty years for one lesson! How slow, and how patient. No university can run on this basis. . . .God goes slowly in his educational process of man. "Forty years in the wilderness" points to his basic educational philosophy.[4]

Biblical characters illustrate the humility needed to submit to God's long-term purposes: Abraham waiting for his promised son and then being willing to offer him up as a sacrifice; John the Baptist living an ascetic life in the wilderness; Paul the apostle maintaining winning attitudes while in prison.

Highly esteemed leaders of our age also teach us humility. Mother Theresa's willingness to care for societal rejects and the dying; Bible translators who work for years in obscurity; urban workers who risk their lives daily in the cause of Christ—all of these people teach us what it is to be humble.

Consider the Outcome: Sacrifice and Suffering

The greatest of leaders are often the ones marked by hardship, bearing on their bodies and soul—like Paul the apostle—the "brandmarks" of Jesus.

Joseph Tson's brandmarks came as a Christian leader in his home country of Romania. Before being exiled, Tson was imprisoned, brought in for questioning frequently, and routinely harassed. Under his leadership, his Baptist church grew to be one of the largest in Romania. People followed him because he was willing to suffer with them and for them.

When asked about the church in the United States, Joseph Tson applauds our generosity and openness, but he fears our aversion to hardship. "Everywhere I go," Tson said, "I ask people to introduce me as 'Joseph Tson, a *slave* of Jesus Christ.' Inevitably, I am introduced as a 'servant' or a 'minister' or a 'worker' of Jesus Christ, but no one wants to call me a slave—perhaps because being a slave connotes ownership or harsh treatment. I fear Christian faith where we are not willing to be *slaves* for Christ. If He suffered for us, should we expect less as His followers, His slaves?"[5]

From Tson we learn that the gospel means suffering, and we must ask ourselves if we are willing to follow. We evaluate Paul's comment to Timothy that "in fact, everyone who wants to live a godly life in Christ Jesus will be persecuted" (2 Timothy 3:12), and we must ask if we will rise to the challenge of that kind of leadership.

As we consider the outcome of the life of faith in older leaders, we soon realize that many have suffered deeply. Elisabeth Elliot writes poignantly and insightfully about pain and loneliness because she has lost one husband to cancer and another to the spears of the Auca Indians.

Bill Walton, one of the original founders of the Holiday Inn hotel chain, lost money and a chance to be chairman of the board because of his Christian convictions. One writer, holding Bill up as an exemplary Christian in business, concluded that "Bill Walton is a marketplace mentor who has learned the hard way that the rose garden of success is bristling with thorns that can bleed a person dry apart from the Lord's help."[6]

Leighton and Jean Ford learned suffering anew when their son, Sandy, died in 1981. With a fresh perspective on the meaning of the cross, Ford writes:

> I am afraid too many of us, especially in the West today, want a Christ without a cross, a Savior who will fulfill us, but not call us to suffering. Yet we are called not just to receive Jesus as Savior, but to follow Him as Lord and the way of the cross.[7]

If we study the lives of older leaders—of our time or of previous times—we will find the brandmarks of Jesus imprinted on their lives. Then we will be honestly confronted afresh with the realities of following Christ.

Consider the Outcome: Endurance

One of the themes of this book has been perseverance or endurance. Why? Because we who are young often want quick results in short periods of time. Like the Hebrews, we "need to persevere so that when you have done the will of God, you will receive what he has promised" (Hebrews 10:36).

Paderewski, the great violinist, was called a genius by an admiring fan. "Perhaps I am," he responded, "but before I was a genius I was a drudge."[8] Are we willing to be "drudges" in our younger years so that we have "genius" in our later years?

World history is full of leaders whose impact was directly related to their perseverance. Sir Walter Scott overcame his crippled state; George Washington endured against overwhelming obstacles (both his enemies and the weather); Abraham Lincoln fought against abject poverty and multiple defeats in government; Franklin D. Roosevelt was struck down with infantile paralysis. The leaders who overcame physical handicaps, racial prejudice, and economic hardships inspire us to persevere.

In the same way, Christian leaders who have had the most significant impact on our world have been those that endured. "Stick-to-it-iveness" is often the key issue that distinguishes Christian leaders. This is as true of Samuel Zwemer, who toiled with Muslim evangelism for forty seemingly fruitless years, as it is of the innumerable men and women (known only by God and a few others) who toil faithfully,

- as lay leaders in struggling churches,
- as pastor/farmers in rural outreach missions,
- as Christian parents seeking to disciple their children,
- as business or community leaders seeking to make an impact for Christ,
- as missionaries on the city dumps of Cairo, Manila, or Tijuana.

Oswald Sanders describes the endurance that leaders need (and that he has personally exemplified!) in *Spiritual Leadership*:

> If he is not willing to rise earlier and stay up later than others, to work harder and study more diligently than his contemporaries, he will not greatly impress his generation. If he is unwilling to pay the price of fatigue for his leadership, it will always be mediocre.[9]

By my desk, I have a framed portion of a poem by Longfellow. These words challenge me to endure:

> The heights by great men reached and kept
> Were not attained by sudden flight,
> But they, while their companions slept,
> Were toiling upward in the night.

Never give up!

LEARN FROM THEIR SUCCESSES

Older leaders provide us with models of effectiveness in ministry in addition to their example of Christlike character. Older men and women in leadership teach us that success is related more to sustained growth than to "flash in the pan" fame or notoriety.

While speaking of athletic fitness, Bill Cosby illustrates a principle that young people can apply to spiritual health: "I have come to realize that if a person sustained some of this [physical] intensity after his college days, he would be in better shape in his 40's or 50's."[10] Those who are overweight at age forty-five usually did not become so overnight; it was probably a gradual addition of one or two pounds per year for fifteen or twenty years. The habits of our younger adult years yield results later in life.

The same is true in our desire for spiritual success. We learn from the lives of older leaders that the habits we form now will shape our future. Albert Schweitzer was famous as an interpreter of Bach, had written a classic in theology, and had achieved great wealth. His successes, however, did not cause him to rest on his achievements. Instead, he left it all at age forty to go into the interior of equatorial Africa to serve as a missionary.[11] Whether we agree with Schweitzer's theology or not, we can admire his sustained commitment to growth.

The older leaders to be emulated are those that sustain their growth as well as their leadership. To be able to thrive through all of life's changes and in the face of all of life's difficulties is the greatest success. We should look for older leaders whose example we can follow.

LEARN FROM THEIR FAILURES

Rebuilding Your Broken World is Gordon MacDonald's book about rebounding from failure. It should be required reading for every young leader because it teaches us that we are all vulnerable to the bad decisions or hurtful priorities that can damage or destroy our marriages, our ministries, and our abilities to lead others.

I admire Gordon MacDonald because—even though he stumbled—he got back up! I admire Charles Blair for the same reason. He tells his story in *The Man Who Could Do No Wrong* and uses his failure to teach us how to avoid pitfalls.

As students of older leaders, we will watch some succeed and others fail, but we can learn from both. From some, we will see defensiveness, the unwillingness to admit error, and the sad fight to protect an image or a ministry empire. From others, we will see humility, the willingness to say, "I failed; please forgive me," and the decided effort to get back on their feet.

Both types should challenge us to ask, "How can I avoid the same failures?" and "When I do fail, will I respond with humility and a repentant spirit?"

CHOOSING A MENTOR

Of all the resources young leaders can draw upon, this last resource, older leaders, is the most strategic. We can shape our ministries, add to our wisdom, and grow beyond our limited experience if we choose good mentors.

Learn from Reading

Throughout this book, I have used multiple quotations from John R.W. Stott, Charles Haddon Spurgeon, D. Martyn Lloyd-Jones, J. Oswald Sanders, and others. In my own growth, these and other writers have served as Christian mentors. Although I have never had the privilege of being personally discipled by these leaders, they have had a profound effect on me through their writings.

By reading biographies, books about leadership, and other Christian literature, we can be mentored by those who have led the Church through the ages. Reading can affect us again and again, in the privacy of personal study, especially as we go back to the spiritual classics of our time and before. We are all challenged to grow as we expose ourselves to the mentoring words of older leaders, such as these from Sanders's *Spiritual Leadership*:

> The young man of leadership caliber will work while others waste time, study while

> others sleep, pray while others play. There will be no place for loose or slovenly habits in word or thought, deed or dress. He will observe a soldierly discipline in diet and deportment, so that he might wage a good warfare. He will without reluctance undertake the unpleasant task which others avoid, or the hidden duty which others evade because it evokes no applause or wins no appreciation. A Spirit-filled leader will not shrink from facing up to difficult situations or persons, or from grasping the nettle when that is necessary. He will kindly and courageously administer rebuke when that is called for; or he will exercise necessary discipline when the interests of the Lord's work demand it. He will not procrastinate in writing the difficult letter. His letter-basket will not conceal the evidences of his failure to grapple with urgent problems.[12]

Go After Mentors

Joshua set a good example for us as a young leader. His mentor, Moses, would speak with the Lord "face to face, as a man speaks with his friend," and Joshua, Moses' young aide, "did not leave [Moses'] tent" (Exodus 33:11). Joshua put himself in the position where he could learn constantly from Moses and observe his relationship with the Lord.

Don, a corporate executive with an ITT company, was known throughout the company for his Christian character. I asked him how he had developed as a Christian leader in a competitive environment. He explained it in one sentence: "I chose a good mentor." His mentor exemplified Christian character in the business world, and Don developed his own leadership style around that example.

John Stott was asked, "How does one become a great preacher?" He answered, "Listen to great preaching!"[13] Go after the communicators who are both true to the Word and relevant to the world, and emulate them. (We have the privilege of going after preaching mentors in wonderful ways in this age of audio and videotapes!)

A young seminary student had lunch with J. I. Packer, theologian and author of many books, including *Knowing God*. After the meal, I asked him what he learned. "Nothing much," replied the seminarian. "I couldn't think of anything to ask." A growth opportunity was wasted because he did not pursue the wisdom of this older Christian leader!

I wanted to learn something about writing, so I signed up for a course with Elisabeth Elliot. I wanted to learn preaching, so I sat under the teaching of Gordon MacDonald and pursued opportunities to hear Roberta Hestenes, Tony Campolo, Haddon Robinson, Billy Graham, and others. I needed to learn about world missions, so I corresponded with leaders in the field.

Some will respond, "But these folks are so busy. I

don't want to trouble them with my questions." My answer to that objection is twofold. First, it cannot hurt to try; if we write and never get a response, we can still learn by listening to tapes, hearing messages at conferences, or reading books. Second, we need not confine ourselves to the "big names." I have learned prayer, interpersonal relationships, forgiveness, and grace from older Christian leaders who never speak at conferences or write books. The criterion for choosing mentors should be Christlikeness, not fame.

Ask Questions

At age twelve, Jesus was found in the Temple courts, "sitting among the teachers . . . asking them questions" (Luke 2:46). As a young man, Jesus exemplified a hunger to learn, and His hunger was manifested in the questions He asked of the older religious experts of that day.

Our lives should be characterized by that same inquiring spirit. Someone has said, "When I am talking, I am not learning anything new." We grow most by asking questions and learning from others.

Questions to mentors can range widely, from "How did you become a Christian?" to "What would you do in this situation?" Whatever the question, we can learn from the experiences of leadership veterans. (Other useful questions appear under "Invite Critique.")

Realize Their Fallibility

Mentors are key resources for our growth as young leaders, but our faith should not rest on these mentors.

We follow Jesus, and these men and women serve as catalysts toward that end. Paul Moede summarizes it well in *Discipleship Journal*:

> If we put our disciplers on a pedestal, we imply that they are infallible. That is unfair to the discipler and disastrous to the disciple. The tragedy of Jonestown is only the most graphic and stunning example of this error.
>
> I will never forget one teacher. I loved being in her class, and staying after school was no punishment. Often I stuck around to help clean erasers, straighten cabinets, and try to be helpful. In my eyes, she could do no wrong.
>
> Then one Saturday morning I saw her in the grocery store, sloppily dressed and smoking. For me, at ten years old, it was devastating. My heroine had a weakness!
>
> Trust your discipler. Respect him. But don't expect infallibility. Don't be shocked at common personal weakness. Above all, don't put him on God's throne.[14]

Invite Critique

The degree to which we learn from our mentors is directly proportional to the feedback we receive and the accountability we experience. If we desire to grow from the wisdom of others, we must ask them to offer us "faithful wounds" (Proverbs 27:6, NASB), which will confront us with our weaknesses.

In *Rebuilding Your Broken World*, Gordon MacDonald suggests twenty-six questions to help develop accountability and invite feedback. If we desire to grow, we should submit ourselves to a spiritual mentor and answer these questions honestly.

1. How is your relationship with God right now?
2. What have you read in the Bible in the past week?
3. What has God said to you in this reading?
4. Where do you find yourself resisting Him these days?
5. What specific things are you praying for in regard to others?
6. What specific things are you praying for in regard to yourself?
7. What are the specific tasks facing you right now that you consider incomplete?
8. What habits intimidate you?
9. What have you read in the secular press this week?
10. What general reading are you doing?
11. What have you done to play?
12. How are you doing with your spouse? Kids?
13. If I were to ask your spouse about your state of mind, state of spirit, state of energy level, what would the response be?
14. Are you sensing spiritual attacks from the enemy right now?

15. If Satan were to try to invalidate you as a person or as a servant of the Lord, how might he do it?
16. What is the state of your sexual perspective? Tempted? Dealing with fantasies? Entertainment?
17. Where are you financially right now? (things under control? under anxiety? in great debt?)
18. Are there any unresolved conflicts in your circle of relationships right now?
19. When was the last time you spent time with a good friend of your own gender?
20. What kind of time have you spent with anyone who is a non-Christian this month?
21. What challenges do you think you're going to face in the coming week? Month?
22. What would you say are your fears at this present time?
23. Are you sleeping well?
24. What three things are you most thankful for?
25. Do you like yourself at this point in your pilgrimage?
26. What are your greatest confusions about your relationship with God?[15]

Ask for Responsibility

As we consider the process of being mentored by an older leader, we need to ask for opportunities to learn through leading. A mentor who protects us from failure by keeping us from taking responsibility will actually stunt our growth rather than help it.

John R. Mott, a great leader in the Student Volunteer Movement, exhorted older leaders to invest in younger leaders by "giving them full play and adequate outlet for their powers. In order to achieve that, heavy burdens of responsibility should be laid on them, including increasing opportunities of initiative and power of final decision."[16]

Full growth as a young leader will come as we have leaders with Mott's perspective over us. We will "take up the torch" in the Christian relay only as older leaders are willing to pass it (or at least share it) with us.

Discipleship does not require a spiritual "cloning," where one's individuality is suppressed in an effort to please a mentor. Instead, a godly mentor will encourage us to pursue Christian maturity and responsible leadership within the boundaries of our own unique personalities and gifts.

GO TO THE HOT SPOTS

Fact 1: We obtained a kitten from an animal shelter several years ago. *Fact 2*: The kitten had recently been spayed, so her belly was shaven. *Fact 3:* We keep our winter thermostat at fifty-eight degrees; our house was quite cold. *Fact 4:* I am quite bald. *Fact 5*: As much as forty percent of one's body heat leaves through the head.

All of these facts led to an exciting adventure the first night we had that kitten. A loud purring awakened me about three o'clock in the morning. I opened my eyes to find the little kitten wrapped around my head, her shaven belly on the baldest part of my head.

As I debated my predicament, I thought, "There must be an illustration in this." There is.

We are the kittens, knowing our need for wisdom, growth, and spiritual heat from others—especially older, more resourceful leaders. The world that we serve in is cold and harsh to the gospel, so we must go to the hot spots to find the answers to our needs. There are risks involved in getting help from others, but we must be bold and go after older leaders who can help us rise to the challenges that God gives us.

Conclusion

The Challenge of the Future

As aspiring young leaders, we face a challenge: Will we rise up to take our place in guiding the Church into the twenty-first century? This is no small task for it involves the development of Christlike character as well as resourceful responses to the world we serve.

THE CHALLENGES ARE EXTERNAL

There are more people without knowledge of Christ than ever before. Missionaries, tentmakers, and church-planters are desperately needed to take the gospel to the ends of the earth. Eddie Gibbs writes in *I Believe in Church Growth*, "the church needs a new generation of leaders with a true apostolic gift of the trail-blazing kind."[1]

The need of people to spread the gospel is exaggerated by the moral and ethical crises of our times. People—even many who call themselves Christians—are drifting from the moorings of Christian standards. Prophetic voices are needed to draw people back. Referring to these crises, Ted Engstrom exhorts us to "give of your best in the worst of times."[2]

Beyond these issues, the global context for world mission grows increasingly complex. James A. Scherer, in his book *Gospel, Church and Kingdom*, lists six specific external realities that we will need to address as leaders in the years ahead:

1. Widespread *poverty and starvation* throughout most of the Two-Thirds World, combined with the increasing gap between rich and poor.
2. *Political instability and authoritarian political systems* on both the right and left—especially in the Two-Thirds World.
3. Religious *pluralism*, combined with rampant growth of fanaticism in some ethnic religions will result in increased competition between Christianity and old, established religions.
4. Despite all this, the *Christian community in the Two-Thirds World* will continue to grow, and these Christians—because of severe testing—are likely to have a quality and vigor of faith that will surpass Christians in the secular West.
5. The Christian community in the *North* will experience increasing malaise and loss of dynamism until it eventually commits itself to the process of re-evangelization.
6. Massive *demographic changes* will mark the new era, with the world population rising to 6.25 billion by the year 2000, with the greatest challenge being the enormous *urban* centers.[3]

Scherer concludes, "In the new era of global mission, the movement will be from everywhere to everywhere; every country will be a 'home base,' and every country a 'mission field.'"[4 5]

THE CHALLENGES ARE INTERNAL

In spite of all these external realities, we still find our greatest challenge to be an internal one: to live an exemplary life. Lorne Sanny writes, "There is a shortage of Christian leadership because of the unwillingness to pay the price—and it begins with character."[6]

Until we dedicate ourselves to the cultivation of our personal commitments to Jesus Christ, our leadership will not be sufficient to lead in these difficult times. We cannot lead others into the battle unless we are committed to being examples by our appearance, personality, and attitude.

"Be an example to those who believe" remains our greatest challenge.

WHAT WILL WE DO?

The choice is now ours. Will we rise to the challenge of exemplary leadership? Will we draw on the resources that God has given us to make us adequate to the tasks before us? Will we stand for our convictions?

Myron Rush identifies tough issues facing every Christian leader in *The New Leader*. We are wise to ponder them slowly.

- You must be willing to stand alone.
- You must be willing to go against public opinion in order to promote what you believe.
- You must be willing to risk failure.
- You must become master of your emotions.
- You must strive to remain above reproach.
- You must be willing to make decisions others don't want to make.
- You must be willing to say no at times, even when you'd like to say yes.
- You must sometimes be willing to sacrifice personal interests for the good of the group.
- You must never be content with the average; you must always strive for the best.
- People must be more important to you than possessions.
- You will have to work harder to keep your life in balance than people do who are not leaders.[7]

Do we want to be leaders? There are costs, but the call of God is greater. Stuart Briscoe writes, "The world—and the church—so desperately needs people at this very hour who are committed to a life of godliness and singleness of purpose. . . .Settle for nothing less than a heart for God."[8]

WILL WE DEDICATE OURSELVES TO BEING EQUIPPED?

This is the most significant question we face. We are not adequate. The challenges are too severe. Our character is too flawed to consider exemplary leadership.

But leadership, like Christian growth, is a process. We dedicate ourselves to growth. We say with the hymn-writer Frances Havergal, "Take my life and let it be consecrated, Lord, to Thee."[9] We offer ourselves to Jesus Christ as living sacrifices (Romans 12:1-2), believing that He will equip us. God's purpose is to exalt Himself, not us, and an effective leader is dedicated *first* to exalting Christ in his or her own life.

Oswald J. Smith, pastor of the People's Church of Toronto for many years and prolific writer, prayed on his thirty-eighth birthday that God would make him a man after His own heart. As he prayed, he saw his priorities in a new light:

> I saw as I had never seen before, that the big thing was not the work I was doing, the books I was writing, the sermons I was preaching, the crowds that gathered, nor the success achieved; but rather the life I was living, the thoughts I was thinking, heart holiness, practical righteousness; in a word: my transformation, by the Spirit, into Christlikeness.[10]

Smith's observation caused him to recommit himself to the process of Christian growth. Whatever the external performance, his priority was his inner growth into the image of Christ.

The process of being equipped is seldom easy, but

it is the key to the fulfilled life that Christ has for us. Carefully consider this passage:

When God wants to drill a man
  And thrill a man
  And skill a man,
When God wants to mold a man
  To play the noblest part;
When He yearns with all His heart
  To create so great and bold a man
That all the world shall be amazed,
  Watch His methods, watch His ways!
How He ruthlessly perfects
  Whom He royally elects!
How He hammers him and hurts him,
  And with mighty blows converts him
Into trial shapes of clay
  Which only God understands;
While his tortured heart is crying
  And he lifts beseeching hands!
How He bends but never breaks
  When his good He undertakes;
How He uses whom He chooses
  And with every purpose fuses him;
  By every act induces him
To try His splendor out—
    God knows what He's about![11]

Notes

Challenge for Young Leaders

1. From the newsletter of InterVarsity staff member Douglas Whallon, October 1988.
2. "Postponed generation" is a term from the book by Susan Littwin, *The Postponed Generation* (New York: William Merrow, 1986).
3. Gordon Fee, *U.S. News and World Report*, April 4, 1988, quoted in *Collegiate Trends* (InterVarsity, May 1988, Issue 40), p. 1.
4. M. Scott Peck, *The Road Less Traveled* (New York: Touchstone, 1978), p. 15.
5. Donald McCullough, *Waking from the American Dream* (Downers Grove, Illinois: InterVarsity Press, 1988), p. 66.
6. McCullough, pp. 26-27.
7. Ted Engstrom, *Seizing the Torch* (Ventura, California: Regal, 1988).
8. John R.W. Stott, *Involvement II* (Old Tappan, New Jersey: Fleming H. Revell, 1985), p. 247.

9. Gordon Fee, *1 and 2 Timothy* (New York: Harper & Row, 1984), p. 41.
10. J. Oswald Sanders, *Paul the Leader* (Colorado Springs, Colorado: NavPress, 1984), p. 185.
11. Luis Palau, in his message at LEADERSHIP 88 in Washington, D.C., July 1, 1988.
12. Gordon MacDonald, *Re-Discovering Yourself* (Old Tappan, New Jersey: Fleming H. Revell, 1985), p. 198.
13. Kent and Barbara Hughes, *Liberating Ministry from the Success Syndrome* (Wheaton, Illinois: Tyndale, 1987), p. 41.
14. Ted Engstrom, *The Making of a Christian Leader* (Grand Rapids: Zondervan, 1976), p. 120.

Part One

1. John R. W Stott, *Between Two Worlds* (Grand Rapids: Eerdmans, 1982), p. 78.
2. Ajith Fernando, *Leadership Lifestyle* (Wheaton, Illinois: Tyndale, 1986), p. 101.
3. Tony Campolo, *The Power Delusion* (Wheaton, Illinois: Victor, 1983), pp. 76-77.
4. Kenneth Leech, *Soul Friend* (New York: Harper & Row, 1977), p. 42.
5. C.S. Lewis, *The Four Loves* (London: Fontana, 1958), pp. 128.
6. From a personal conversation with J. Oswald Sanders, March 11, 1988.
7. Leighton Ford, in his message at LEADERSHIP 88, June 27, 1988.

8. Donald McCullough, *Waking from the American Dream* (Downers Grove, Illinois: InterVarsity Press, 1988), p. 134.
9. From an article by Peter Petre on Kenneth Olsen in *Fortune*, October 27, 1986, p. 32.
10. Thomas Ken, "Awake My Soul," *Hymns II* (Downers Grove, Illinois: InterVarsity Press, 1976), p. 181.

CHAPTER 1

1. Leighton Ford's introduction of Glandion Carney at LEADERSHIP 88, June 27, 1988.
2. Charles Spurgeon, *Lectures to My Students* (Grand Rapids: Zondervan, 1972), p. 19.
3. Quoted in J. Oswald Sanders "The Prayers of a Leader," *Discipleship Journal* (Issue 41, 1987), p. 36.
4. Kent and Barbara Hughes, *Liberating Ministry from the Success Syndrome* (Wheaton, Illinois: Tyndale, 1987), p. 78.
5. Gary Smalley and John Trent, *The Blessing* (Nashville: Thomas Nelson, 1986). This is the theme of the book.
6. Eugene B. Habecker, *The Other Side of Leadership* (Wheaton, Illinois: Victor, 1987), p. 179.
7. Carole Mayhall, *Words that Hurt, Words that Heal* (Colorado Springs, Colorado: NavPress, 1986), p. 46.

8. Richard Baxter, *The Reformed Pastor* (Carlisle, Pennsylvania: Banner of Truth Trust, 1974), p. 63.
9. Thomas Carlyle, quoted in Ted Engstrom, *Seizing the Torch* (Ventura, California: Regal, 1988), p. 116.
10. Gordon MacDonald, *Rebuilding Your Broken World* (Nashville: Oliver-Nelson, 1988), p. 192.
11. D. Martyn Lloyd-Jones, *Preaching and Preachers* (Grand Rapids: Baker, 1971), p. 166.
12. John R.W. Stott, *The Preacher's Portrait* (Grand Rapids: Eerdmans, 1961), p. 75.
13. Engstrom, *Seizing the Torch,* p. 105.
14. Paraphrase of Chad Walsh, *Campus Gods on Trial* (New York: Macmillan, 1953), p. 95.
15. Bill Hybels, *Who You Are When No One's Looking* (Downers Grove, Illinois: InterVarsity Press, 1987), p. 70.
16. Mayhall, p. 49.
17. J. Oswald Sanders, *Spiritual Leadership* (Chicago: Moody Press, 1967), p. 60.
18. *Latin America Evangelist* (Coral Gables, Florida: Latin America Mission), May-June, 1965, p. 5.

CHAPTER 2

1. Robert Raines, *Creative Brooding* (New York: Macmillan, 1966).
2. Harold Myra ed., *Leaders* (Carol Stream, Illinois: CTI/Word, 1987), pp. 52-53.

3. Ted Engstrom, *Integrity* (Waco, Texas: Word, 1987), p. 92.
4. Charles Spurgeon, *Lectures to My Students* (Grand Rapids: Zondervan, 1972), p. 17.
5. Paul Tournier, *Creative Suffering* (New York: Harper & Row, 1983), p. 5.
6. John R. W. Stott, *The Preacher's Portrait* (Grand Rapids: Eerdmans, 1961), p. 30.
7. Bill Hybels, "But I'm an Exception," *Leadership Magazine* (Spring 1988, Vol. 9, No. 2), p. 37.
8. Tournier, p. 29.
9. Viktor Frankl, quoted in Gordon MacDonald, *Re-Discovering Yourself* (Old Tappan, New Jersey: Fleming H. Revell, 1985) p. 209.
10. From the introduction to an interview with Mark Hatfield in *Leadership Magazine* (Spring 1988, Vol. 9, No. 2), p. 128.
11. Quoted in Kent and Barbara Hughes, *Liberating Ministry from the Success Syndrome* (Wheaton, Illinois: Tyndale, 1987), p. 186.
12. Gary Inrig, *A Call to Excellence* (Wheaton, Illinois: Victor, 1985), p. 87.
13. Brian Harbour, *Rising Above the Crowd* (Nashville: Broadman, 1988), p. 9.
14. Sammy Tippit, *Fire in Your Heart* (Chicago: Moody Press, 1987), p. 26.
15. Spurgeon, p. 12.
16. Robert Murray McCheyne, quoted in Stott, *The Preacher's Portrait*, p. 120.
17. Paul Lee Tan, *Encyclopedia of 7700 Illustrations* (Garland, Texas: Assurance, 1984), p. 735.

CHAPTER 3

1. Quoted in Susan Littwin, *The Postponed Generation* (New York: William Merrow, 1986), p. 35.
2. Donald McCullough, *Waking from the American Dream* (Downers Grove, Illinois: InterVarsity Press, 1988), p. 44.
3. Elisabeth Elliot, quoted in *Discipleship Journal* (Issue 41, 1987), p. 25.
4. J. Oswald Sanders, *Spiritual Leadership* (Chicago: Moody Press, 1967), p. 17.
5. Charles Williams, *The Place of the Lion* (Grand Rapids: Eerdmans, 1974), p. 74.
6. A.W Tozer, *Knowledge of the Holy* (New York: Harper & Row 1961), p. 10.
7. Amy Carmichael, quoted in Sanders, *Spiritual Leadership*, p. 106.
8. C.S. Lewis, *The Four Loves* (London: Fontana, 1958), pp.138-139.
9. Bill Hybels, *Who You Are When No One's Looking* (Downers Grove, Illinois: InterVarsity Press, 1987), p. 64.
10. Milton Friesen, in his message at the Grace Chapel Missions Conference, April 16, 1986.
11. Evelyn Underhill, *Concerning the Inner Life* (Minneapolis: Seabury Press, n.d.), p. 101.
12. George Appleton, *The Oxford Book of Prayer* (New York: Oxford University Press, 1985), p. 81.
13. Tony Campolo, *The Success Fantasy* (Wheaton, Illinois: Victor, 1986), p. 20.

14. Tony Campolo, *The Power Delusion* (Wheaton, Illinois: Victor, 1983), p. 159.
15. Michael Griffiths, *What on Earth Are You Doing?* (Grand Rapids: Baker, 1983), p. 56.

Chapter 4

1. Franklin Roosevelt, quoted in Ted Engstrom, *Seizing the Torch* (Ventura, California: Regal, 1988), p. 144.
2. John Henry Jowett, quoted in Gary Inrig, *A Call to Excellence* (Wheaton, Illinois. Victor, 1985), p. 51.
3. Bill Hybels, *Who You Are When No One's Looking* (Downers Grove, Illinois. InterVarsity Press, 1987), p. 14.
4. Peter Lord, in his message at the Reach Out National Evangelism Leadership Conference at Ridgecrest, North Carolina, April 1981.
5. Thomas á Kempis, *The Imitation of Christ* (Chicago: Moody Press, n.d.), p. 12.
6. A.W. Tozer, *That Incredible Christian* (Harrisburg, Pennsylvania: Christian Publications, 1964), p. 27.
7. Charles Blair, *The Man Who Could Do No Wrong* (Lincoln, Virginia: Chosen Books, 1981), p. 233.
8. Tony Campolo, *The Power Delusion* (Wheaton, Illinois: Victor, 1983), p. 57.
9. Terry Muck, *When to Take a Risk* (Carol Stream, Illinois: CTI/Word, 1987), p. 33.

10. David M. Howard, *What Makes a Missionary?* (Chicago: Moody Press, 1987), p. 74.
11. Michael Griffiths, *What on Earth Are You Doing?* (Grand Rapids: Baker, 1983), p. 20.
12. Hudson Taylor, source unknown.
13. E. Stanley Jones, *A Song of Ascents* (Nashville: Abingdon, 1968), p. 383.
14. Gordon MacDonald, *Rebuilding Your Broken World* (Nashville: Oliver-Nelson, 1988), p. 47.
15. Kent and Barbara Hughes, *Liberating Ministry from the Success Syndrome* (Wheaton, Illinois: Tyndale, 1987), p. 70.
16. Betty Lee Skinner, *Daws* (Colorado Springs, Colorado: NavPress, 1974, 1987), p. 46.
17. Chua Wee Hian, *The Making of a Leader* (Downers Grove, Illinois: InterVarsity Press, 1987), p. 94.
18. Paul Tournier, *Creative Suffering* (New York: Harper & Row, 1983), pp. 1-3.
19. Griffiths, p. 66.
20. Tozer, p. 116.
21. Charles Swindoll, *A Quest for Character* (Portland, Oregon: Multnomah, 1987), p. 98.

CHAPTER 5

1. Charles Colson, in his address at LEADERSHIP 88, June 29, 1988.
2. *U.S. News and World Report*, April 6, 1987, p. 58.

3. "A Nation of Liars?" *U.S. News and World Report*, February 23, 1987, p. 54.
4. Sophie de la Haye, *Byang Kato* (Achimota, Ghana: African Christian Press, 1986), p. 11.
5. Kent and Barbara Hughes, *Liberating Ministry from the Success Syndrome* (Wheaton, Illinois. Tyndale, 1987), p. 92.
6. Eugene B. Habecker, *The Other Side of Leadership* (Wheaton, Illinois: Victor, 1987), p. 185.
7. Richard Foster, *Money, Sex and Power* (New York: Harper & Row, 1985), p. 13.
8. Ted Engstrorn, *Seizing the Torch* (Ventura, California: Regal, 1988), p. 98.
9. Quoted in Catherine Marshall, *Beyond Our Selves* (New York: McGraw-Hill, 1961), pp. 77-78.
10. John R. W Stott, *Involvement II* (Old Tappan, N.J.: Fleming H. Revell, 1985), p. 166.
11. Patti Roberts, *Ashes to Gold* (Waco, Texas: Word, 1983), p. 108.
12. From the hymn, "Come, Thou Fount," *Inspiring Hymns* (Grand Rapids: Singspiration, 1951), p. 405.
13. Hughes, p. 87.
14. From a personal note from a friend.

CHAPTER 6

1. J.C. Ryle, *Holiness* (Grand Rapids: Evangelical Press, 1956), p. 35.

2. Charles H. Spurgeon, *Lectures to My Students* (Grand Rapids: Zondervan, 1972), p. 305.
3. John White, *Excellence in Leadership* (Downers Grove, Illinois: InterVarsity Press, 1986), pp. 47-48.
4. John R.W Stott, *Involvement II* (Old Tappan, New Jersey: Fleming H. Revell, 1985), p. 252.
5. Robert Banks, *The Tyranny of Time* (Downers Grove, Illinois: InterVarsity Press, 1983), p. 144.
6. Banks, p. 66.
7. Paul Tournier, quoted in Banks, p. 40.
8. Robert Bretall, ed., *A Kierkegaard Anthology* (New York: The Modern Library, 1946), p. 271.
9. D. Martyn Lloyd-Jones, *Preaching and Preachers* (Grand Rapids: Baker, 1971), p. 97.
10. Banks, p. 58.
11. Brother Lawrence, *The Practice of the Presence of God* (Old Tappan, New Jersey: Fleming H. Revell, 1958).

Chapter 7

1. Adolphe Monod, quoted in Ted Engstrom, *Seizing the Torch* (Ventura, California: Regal, 1988), p. 134.
2. Source unknown.
3. Joseph Bayly, in a message at a Christian Education Conference at Grace Chapel, November 1978.
4. Leighton Ford, quoted in Engstrom, pp. 206-207.
5. Quoted in John R.W. Stott, *Between Two Worlds* (Grand Rapids: Eerdmans, 1982), p. 59.

6. Billy Graham, *World Evangelization* (December 1986), p. 3.
7. David M. Howard, *What Makes a Missionary?* (Chicago: Moody Press, 1987), p. 14.

Chapter 8

1. Arthur Levine, *When Dreams and Heroes Died* (San Francisco: Jossey-Bass, 1980).
2. John R.W. Stott, *Involvement II* (Old Tappan, New Jersey: Fleming H. Revell, 1985), p. 263.
3. Stuart Briscoe, *David: A Heart for God* (Wheaton, Illinois: Victor, 1988), pp. 110-111.
4. A.W. Tozer, *That Incredible Christian* (Harrisburg, Pennsylvania: Christian Publications, 1964), p. 64.
5. Susan Littwin, *The Postponed Generation* (New York: William Morrow, 1986), p. 64.
6. Littwin, p. 16.
7. Jon Johnston, *Christian Excellence* (Grand Rapids: Baker, 1985), p. 33.
8. Fred Smith, *Learning to Lead* (Carol Stream, Illinois: CTI/Word, 1986), p. 35.
9. Hudson Taylor, source unknown.
10. Stott, p. 264.
11. Ted Engstrom, *Seizing the Torch* (Ventura, California: Regal, 1988), p. 162.
12. Quoted in Waylon Moore, *Multiplying Disciples* (Colorado Springs, Colorado: NavPress, 1981), p. 104.
13. Littwin, p. 15.

14. Elisabeth Elliot, *Shadow of the Almighty* (Grand Rapids: Zondervan, 1958).
15. Mark Hatfield, *Conflict and Conscience* (Waco, Texas: Word, 1971), p. 127.
16. Brian Harbour, *Rising Above the Crowd* (Nashville: Broadman, 1988), p. 26-27.

CHAPTER 9

1. Bill Cosby, *Time Flies* (New York: Doubleday, 1987), p. 100.
2. Ted Engstrom, *Seizing the Torch* (Ventura, California: Regal, 1988), p. 11.
3. Soren Kierkegaard, *Attack Upon Christendom* (Princeton, New Jersey: Princeton University Press, 1968), p. 195.
4. Kosuke Koyama, *The Three Mile An Hour God* (London: SCM, 1979), pp. 3,6-7.
5. From a personal conversation with Joseph Tson at Urbana 87, December 29, 1987.
6. Mel Lorentzen, "Holiday Inn Co-founder William B. Walton: Making Room For God," *Marketplace Networks* (March 1988), p. 5.
7. Leighton Ford, quoted in Engstrom, *Seizing the Torch*, p. 209.
8. Ted Engstrom, *The Pursuit of Excellence* (Grand Rapids: Zondervan, 1982), p. 81.
9. J. Oswald Sanders, *Spiritual Leadership* (Chicago: Moody Press, 1967), p. 109.
10. Cosby, p. 129.

11. Tony Campolo, *The Success Fantasy* (Wheaton, Illinois: Victor, 1986), p. 82.
12. Sanders, p. 45.
13. From a personal conversation with John Stott at a seminar on preaching at Grace Chapel, June 1975.
14. Paul Moede, "Go For the Gusto," *Discipleship Journal* (Issue 30, 1985), p. 30.
15. Gordon MacDonald, *Rebuilding Your Broken World* (Nashville: Oliver-Nelson, 1988), pp. 203-204.
16. Quoted in J. Oswald Sanders, *Paul the Leader* (Colorado Springs, Colorado: NavPress, 1984), p. 179.

Conclusion

1. Eddie Gibbs, *I Believe in Church Growth* (London: Hodder and Stoughton, 1985), p. 247.
2. Ted Engstrom, *Integrity* (Waco, Texas: Word, 1987), p. 108.
3. James A. Scherer, *Gospel, Church and Kingdom* (Minneapolis: Augsburg, 1987), pp. 41-47.
4. Author's Note: Scherer was not far off in his estimation of the world population by the year 2000. According to Operation World (Patrick Johnstone and Jason Mandryk, 2001. (Authentic Media)) the world population in 2000 was 6.06 billion.
5. Scherer, p. 47.

6. Lorne Sanny, in *Discipleship Journal* (Issue 41, 1987), p. 27.
7. Myron Rush, *The New Leader* (Wheaton, Illinois: Victor, 1987), p. 39.
8. Stuart Briscoe, *David: A Heart for God* (Wheaton, Illinois: Victor, 1988), p. 170.
9. Frances R. Havergal, "Take My Life and Let It Be Consecrated," *Hymns for the Family of God* (Nashville: Paragon, 1976), p. 458.
10. Oswald J. Smith, *The Man God Uses* (London: Marshall, Morgan and Scott, 1970), p. 124.
11. Quoted in J. Oswald Sanders, *Spiritual Leadership* (Chicago: Moody Press, 1967), p. 141.

Appendix A

Literature for Leaders

Devotion to the discipline of study must characterize any who aspire to leadership, so resources for further study in leadership and the challenges facing leaders are offered below.

Aldrich, Joseph C. *Life-Style Evangelism.* Portland, Oregon: Multnomah Press, 1983.

Barnett, Jake. *Wealth and Wisdom.* Colorado Springs, Colorado: NavPress, 1987.

Berkley, James D. *Making the Most of Mistakes.* Waco, Texas: Word, Inc., 1987.

Blamires, Harry. *Recovering the Christian Mind.* Downers Grove, Illinois: InterVarsity Press, 1988.

Briscoe, Stuart. *David: A Heart for God.* Wheaton, Illinois. Victor Books, 1988.

Bruce, A.B. *The Training of the Twelve.* Grand Rapids: Kregel Publications, 1979.

Campolo, Anthony, Jr. *The Power Delusion.* Wheaton, Illinois: Victor Books, 1983.

_______. *The Success Fantasy.* Wheaton, Illinois: Victor Books, 1980.

_______. *Who Switched the Price Tags?* Waco, Texas: Word, Inc.,1986.

Chua Wee Hian. *The Making of a Leader*. Downers Grove, Illinois: InterVarsity Press, 1987.

Clouse, Robert G., ed. *Wealth and Poverty*. Downers Grove, Illinois: InterVarsity Press, 1984.

Coleman, Robert E. *The Master Plan of Discipleship*. Old Tappan, New Jersey: Fleming H. Revell, 1987.

Colson, Charles. *Kingdoms in Conflict*. Grand Rapids: Zondervan Publishing House, 1987.

_______. *Loving God*. Grand Rapids: Zondervan Publishing House,1983.

Dayton, Edward R., and Ted Engstrom. *Strategy for Leadership*. Old Tappan, New Jersey: Fleming H. Revell, 1979.

Eims, LeRoy. *Be the Leader You Were Meant to Be*. Wheaton, Illinois: Victor Books, 1979.

Elliot, Elisabeth. *Discipline: The Glad Surrender*. Old Tappan, New Jersey: Fleming H. Revell, 1982.

Engstrom, Ted W. *Integrity*. Waco, Texas: Word, Inc., 1987.

_______. *The Making of a Christian Leader*. Grand Rapids: Zondervan Publishing House, 1979.

_______. *Seizing the Torch*. Ventura, California: Regal Books, 1988.

Foster, Richard J. *Celebration of Discipline*. New York: Harper & Row, Publishers, 1978.

_______. *Money, Sex and Power*. New York: Harper & Row, Publishers, 1987.

Gardner, John W. *Self-Renewal.* New York: Harper & Row, Publishers, 1964.

Habecker, Eugene B. *The Other Side of Leadership.* Wheaton, Illinois: Victor Books, 1987.

Haggai, John. *The Leading Edge.* Waco, Texas: Word, Inc., 1988.

Harbour, Brian L. *Rising Above the Crowd.* Nashville: Broadman Press, 1988.

Hybels, Bill. *Who You Are When No One's Looking.* Downers Grove, Illinois: InterVarsity Press, 1987.

Inrig, Gary. *A Call to Excellence.* Wheaton, Illinois: Victor Books, 1985.

Kempis, Thomas á. *The Imitation of Christ.* Chicago: Moody Press, 1984.

Klay, Robin Kendrick. *Counting the Cost.* Grand Rapids: William B. Eerdmans, 1986.

Law, William. *A Serious Call to a Devout and Holy Life.* Wilton, Connecticut: Morehouse-Barlow, 1982.

MacDonald, Gordon. *Facing Turbulent Times.* Wheaton, Illinois: Tyndale House Publishers, 1981.

_______. *Ordering Your Private World.* Nashville: Thomas Nelson, 1985.

_______. *Rebuilding Your Broken World.* Nashville: Thomas Nelson, 1988.

Mayhall, Carole. *Words that Hurt, Words that Heal.* Colorado Springs, Colorado: NavPress, 1986.

Minirth, Frank, et al. *The Workaholic and His Family.* Grand Rapids: Baker Book House, 1985.

Muck, Terry. *When to Take a Risk.* Waco, Texas: Word, Inc., 1987.

Murray, Andrew. *With Christ in the School of Prayer.* Springdale, Paennsylvania: Whitaker House, 1981.

Petersen, Jim. *Living Proof.* Colorado Springs, Colorado: NavPress, 1989.

Phillips, J.B. *The Price of Success.* Wheaton, Illinois: Harold Shaw Publishers, 1985.

Rush, Myron D. *The New Leader.* Wheaton, Illinois: Victor Books,1987.

Ryle, J.C. *Holiness.* Phillipsburg, New Jersey: Evangelical Press, 1956.

Sanders, J. Oswald. *Spiritual Leadership.* Chicago: Moody Press, 1979.

Sine, Tom. *Why Settle For More and Miss the Best?* Waco, Texas: Word, Inc., 1987.

Smith, David. *The Friendless American Male.* Ventura, California: Regal Books, 1983.

Smith, Fred. *Learning to Lead.* Waco, Texas: Word, Inc., 1986.

_______. *You and Your Network.* Waco, Texas: Word, Inc., 1984.

Spurgeon, Charles H. *Lectures to My Students.* Grand Rapids: Zondervan Publishing House, 1980.

Stafford, Tim. *Knowing the Face of God.* Grand Rapids: Zondervan Publishing House, 1985.

Stott, John R.W *Involvement I and II.* Old Tappan, New Jersey: Fleming H. Revell, 1985.

_______. *The Preacher's Portrait.* Grand Rapids: William B. Eerdmans, 1961.

Swindoll, Charles R. *The Quest for Character.* Portland, Oregon: Multnomah Press, 1987.

Thomas, Cal. *The Death of Ethics in America.* Waco, Texas: Word, Inc., 1988.

Tippit, Sammy. *Fire in Your Heart.* Chicago: Moody Press, 1987.

Tournier, Paul. *Creative Suffering.* New York: Harper & Row, 1983.

Tozer, A.W. *The Knowledge of the Holy.* New York: Harper & Row, 1978.

_______. *The Pursuit of God.* Harrisburg, Pennsylvania: Christian Publications, 1982.

______. *That Incredible Christian.* Harrisburg, Pennsylvania: Christian Publications, 1964.

White, John. *Excellence in Leadership.* Downers Grove, Illinois: InterVarsity Press, 1986.

Yamamori, Tetsunao. *God's New Envoys.* Portland, Oregon: Multnomah Press, 1987.

Youssef, Michael. *The Leadership Style of Jesus.* Wheaton, Illinois: Victor Books, 1986.

Appendix B

Young Leaders' Agenda

[Note: The following was drafted by Gordon Aeschliman and others at the SINGAPORE '87 conference for younger leaders (sponsored by the Lausanne Committee for World Evangelization). Although this document was not officially accepted by the Lausanne Committee, it, like the original Lausanne Covenant, is full of challenges for those who desire to lead in the Church. It is included here for follow-up consideration for those who desire to rise to the challenge of leadership.]

Compelled to love the world because of our deep love for Jesus Christ, we, the United States participants of the Singapore '87 conference, call our generation to humbly and energetically accept responsibility in the task of world evangelization. We commit ourselves to this task in the context of today's world and affirm the Lausanne Covenant.

WORLD EVANGELIZATION TODAY

The advancement of world evangelization is the task

of the whole Church to the whole person for the whole world. This calling necessarily includes the work of evangelism, justice, and mercy.

Christians, having accepted the rule of God in their hearts, now must work for the rule of God in His world. We affirm that Jesus, by His death and resurrection, dealt the final, fatal blow to Satan and announced the arrival of His Kingdom. He established a nation of priests and to them He entrusted the ministry of engaging in battle against the rule of darkness. We weep for societies that live without any knowledge of Christ. We recognize the great challenge of religious systems such as Islam, Hinduism, animism, and secularism, which hold much of our world hostage to deception and unbelief. We accept the gospel imperative of introducing them to the good news.

It is our mandate to extend justice and mercy in the name of the King. We abhor and denounce racism, sexism, religious persecution, and oppressive economic and political systems that deny human beings their dignity. We note specific, contemporary evils such as abortion, apartheid, the suppression of women, Marxism, militant religious fanaticism, an escalating nuclear arms race, world hunger, and unchecked capitalism.

We are aware that the world's urban centers are growing rapidly and call Christians to advance Jesus' love in the cities—to work with the aliens, homeless, hungry, and unemployed who emerge from this global phenomenon.

PARTNERSHIP

We affirm that the world is in a new day of missions and that cooperation with the international Body of Christ is central to the new expression.

We're thankful to God for our own heritage of countless missionaries who have gone to all corners of the world, facing death, disease, and separation from loved ones—going because they were spurred by the conviction that all people should have the opportunity to come into Christ's love.

We hold in high regard those men and women who established thousands of churches, hospitals, universities, and agricultural systems out of a love for human beings they had never met. We consider it a privilege to follow in the footsteps of those saints whose lives of faith and sacrifice will always leave the church uneasy with its own complacency.

We openly acknowledge that our mission heritage is not without its failures. We confess the sin of our participation in structures and ideas that have dominated rather than liberated others. We reject the spirit of cultural superiority and the marriage of our particular political ideology to the Kingdom of God. This unbiblical perspective has at times marred our commitment to justice, blinded us to the truth of equality before God, and allowed us to support both imperialism and oppressive host governments.

We understand that we are co-laborers with God and our brothers and sisters of the Third World in the task of world evangelization. We look forward to the next several decades of ministering together and call for mutuality versus superiority or inferiority; cooperation versus competition or parochialism; servanthood versus manipulation or control. We pray for a humble heart.

In the spirit of full partnership we ask Third World missionaries to help us evangelize North America. We trust God will send many of you as laborers to our region. We will endeavor to send you our best cross-cultural servants and desire to cooperate with you in their training and placement.

UNITY AT HOME

"How good it is when brothers and sisters live together in unity." We affirm that God calls us to be Kingdom seekers rather than empire builders. We call on our generation to put aside unessential internal squabbling and rather engage in a coordinated front against the real enemy. We renounce factionalism as a sin and deterrent to world evangelization, a deadly distraction by the evil one to keep us off course. Denominations, missions, and local churches must renounce competition and seek to work together for the advancement of the Kingdom. We plead for an end to jealousy, striving, and vain glory and assert that world evangelization will require the concerted effort of the whole Church.

STEWARDSHIP

"All the earth is the Lord's and the fullness thereof." We believe that ultimately we have no possessions. Rather, we are committed to a biblical understanding of ownership that simply puts God's creation in our care. He intends those resources to be used for the advancement of His Kingdom, and we accept the responsibility of standing under the scrutiny of His judgment when He returns and calls for an accounting of His wealth. We acknowledge that His ownership extends beyond our bank accounts and assets to our time, abilities, and careers. Our very lives are His, and we will not retreat to safety when we are called to the dangerous.

We reject the flagrant materialism that rules our country. We realize that the lure of power, prestige, and comfort offered by money is a great force. Consequently, we call for sound biblical teaching and personal modeling regarding the Christian walk. We resist the unbiblical notions of the prosperity teaching as being blind and selfish reflections of a cultural value that gives freedom to the unlimited acquisition of wealth while the world suffers to survive. We understand that the seduction of wealth dilutes our compassion for the impoverished.

We appeal for a new commitment to the command, "Seek first the Kingdom of God . . ." and call for Christian generosity and missions giving that literally leaves us depending on Him to "add these other things" to us.

PERSONAL HOLINESS

The nature of our ministry must reflect the person of Jesus Christ. Christian ministers must affirm that anything done either publicly or privately that is inconsistent with the character of Jesus Christ is failure. We pray for a new sensitivity in understanding the seriousness of offending His reputation.

We emphatically appeal for moral purity and the responsible raising and utilization of funds. We call for a renewed commitment to spiritual disciplines—the worship of God, the study of His Word, and intercessory prayer. We realize this may require us to establish new personal priorities. We accept that challenge as an integral part in our conditioning for spiritual warfare. We pray for the renewal of our generation, understanding that only when we place our love for Jesus above all other concerns will we find the motivation, energy, and personal resources we need to reach the world.

COURAGE

In establishing this agenda we call our generation to be courageous, to assume leadership for its future, and to set society's agenda rather than merely respond to it. We point to the sacrificial examples of missionaries originating from countries all over the world and say that surely, by God's grace, we will be able to take the risk of living for the Lord. An increasing number of nations are becoming closed to the gospel, and we must be willing to accept the dangers associated with ministering inside their borders. We are dependent on God for the courage we need and recognize our utter inability to be faithful to the task of world evangelization aside from the empowering of the Holy Spirit.

We do not proceed with a self-pitying spirit but with the words of Jesus in our ears: "No one has left house or brothers or sisters or mothers or fathers or children or lands, for My sake and for the gospel, who will not receive a hundred-fold now in this time . . .with persecutions, and in the age to come, eternal life." Amen.

Other books available from...

PO Box 1047
129 Mobilization Dr
Waynesboro, GA 30830

706-554-1594
1-8MORE-BOOKS
gabriel@omlit.om.org

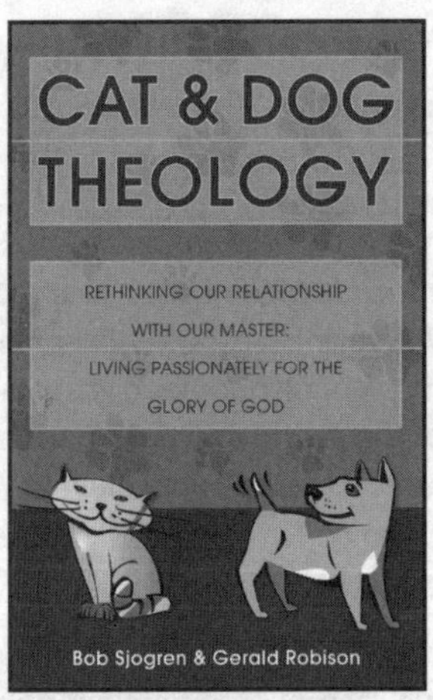

Cat and Dog Theology

Rethinking Our Relationship With Our Master

Bob Sjogren & Dr. Gerald Robison

There is a joke about cats and dogs that conveys their differences perfectly.

> **A dog says, "You pet me, you feed me, you shelter me, you love me, you must be God."**
> **A cat says, "You pet me, you feed me, you shelter me, you love me, I must be God."**

These God-given traits of cats ("You exist to serve me") and dogs ("I exist to serve you") are often similar to the theological attitudes we have in our view of God and our relationship to Him. Using the differences between cats and dogs in a light-handed manner, the authors compel us to challenge our thinking in deep and profound ways. As you are drawn toward God and the desire to reflect His glory in your life, you will worship, view missions, and pray in a whole new way. This life-changing book will give you a new perspective and vision for God as you delight in the God who delights in you.

1884543170 206 Pages

Youth and Missions

Expanding Your Students' World View

Paul Borthwick

188454388X   265 Pages

Youth & Missions is a practical handbook filled with principles, guidelines, and examples of how to help young people to grow in their understanding of the world and their part in it. It provides a basic "step-by-step" approach to:

- motivating youth toward world missions
- modeling world concern
- exposing group members to missions opportunities in the church, youth group, and at home
- providing "life changing" missions experiences
- promoting "long-term" results in students' lives

How to be a World Class Christian

You can be a Part of God's Global Action

Paul Borthwick

1884543227   249 Pages

A world-class Christian is one whose lifestyle and obedience are compatible with what God is doing and wants to be doing in the world. Sound impossible?

Yes, you can be a part of God's global action—from your own neighborhood to the "ends of the earth." As you read and study you will learn:

- What it means to be a world-class Christian
- How you can be a missionary no matter where you live
- Where to get information about worldwide needs and opportunities
- How God is calling you to action now

Lifting the Veil

The World of Muslim Women

Phil and Julie Parshall

1884543677 288 Pages

Secluded from the eyes of anyone but family members, Muslim women live under a system of tradition, rites and rituals that favor men above women. "A man loves first his son, then his camel, and then his wife," says an Arab proverb.

Phil and Julie Parshall bring a sensitive perspective to this thoughtful, yet sobering book that examines the controversy of female circumcision and proof of virginity, the heartache of arranged marriages, divorce, polygamy, and the status of women living in a male dominated world.

This book will not provide you with easy answers but will prompt you to begin praying for these "daughters of Ishmael," and give you sensitive awareness to life behind the veil.

The Cross and The Crescent

Understanding the Muslim Heart and Mind

Phil Parshall

1884543685 320 Pages

Who are the Muslims? You hear about them in the news every day. Many people associate them with terrorism and cruelty. Some admire their willingness to die for their faith. Others wonder if there is more to Islam than fanaticism and martyrdom. And Christians ask, "How do we respond in faith and love to these people?" This question is more pressing than ever.

Phil Parshall understands the Muslim heart and mind. Living as a missionary among Muslims, he knows them - not as a band of fanatics on the evening news, but as individuals, some good, some bad. In this very warm, very personal book he looks at what Muslims believe and how their beliefs affect and often don't affect their behavior. He compares and contrasts Muslim and Christian views on the nature of God, sacred Scriptures, worship, sin and holiness, mysticism, Jesus and Muhammed, human suffering and the afterlife.

God's Great Ambition

A Mega-Motivating Crash Course on God's Heart
Dan and Dave Davidson
and George Verwer
1884543693 208 Pages

This unique collection of quotes and Scriptures has been designed to motivate thousands of people into action in world missions. George Verwer and the Davidsons are well-known for their ministries of mission mobilization as speakers and writers.

Turn to any page and get ready to be encouraged and respond with an increase of awareness, action and ownership in sharing God's good news around His world.

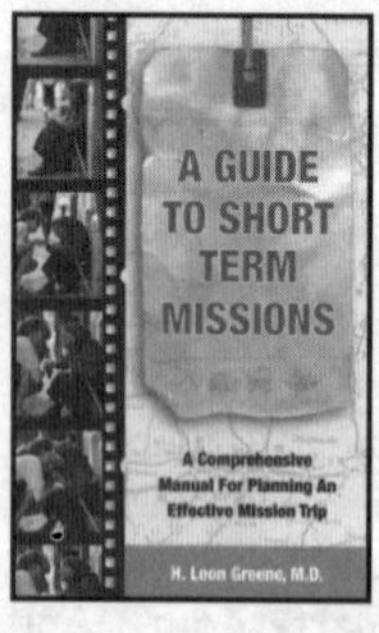

A Guide to Short-Term Missions

A Comprehensive Manual for Planning an Effective Mission Trip
Dr. H. Leon Greene
1884543731 288 Pages

Drawing on his experiences from over thirty short-term mission trips, Dr. Greene gives a detailed look at the challenges and blessings faced by those who are considering such an endeavor. This one-stop guide helps make the most of this opportunity by outlining the steps to take from start to finish. Included are great resources such as:

- Preparing a testimony
- Writing a support letter
- Getting a passport
- Forming the team
- How to stay healthy
- Useful web sites
- Emergency plans & disaster relief
- How and what to prepare for
- Immunizations needed
- Packing checklist
- Other helpful resources

Operation World

Patrick Johnstone & Jason Mandryk

Prayer Calendar

This spiral desk calendar contains clear graphics and useful geographic, cultural, economic, and political statistics on 122 countries of the world. The *Operation World Prayer Calendar* is a great tool to help you pray intelligently for the world. Pray for each country for three days and see how God works!

1884543596 256 Pages

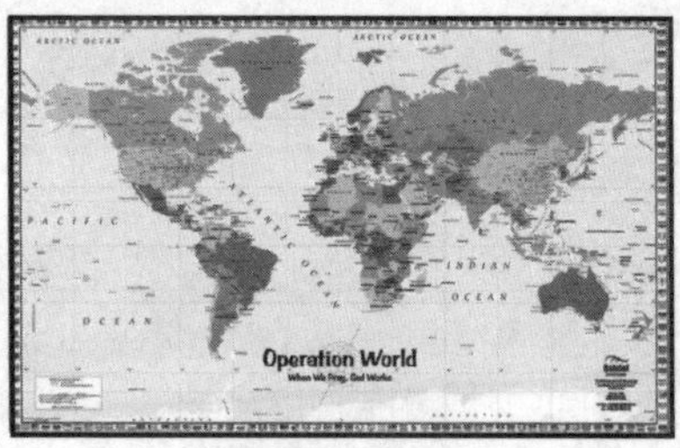

Wall Map

22" x 36"

This beautiful, full-color wall map is a great way to locate the countries that you are praying for each day and build a global picture. Not only an excellent resource for schools, churches, and offices, but a valuable tool for the home.

188454360X Laminated
1884543618 Folded